# The Recovery of Hope

Text copyright © Naomi Starkey 2016
The author asserts the moral right to be identified as the author of this work

**Published by**
**The Bible Reading Fellowship**
15 The Chambers, Vineyard
Abingdon OX14 3FE
United Kingdom
Tel: +44 (0)1865 319700
Email: enquiries@brf.org.uk
Website: www.brf.org.uk
BRF is a Registered Charity

ISBN 978 0 85746 417 0

First published 2016
10 9 8 7 6 5 4 3 2 1 0
All rights reserved

**Acknowledgements**
Scripture quotations are taken from The New Revised Standard Version of the
Bible, Anglicised edition, copyright © 1989, 1995 by the Division of Christian
Education of the National Council of the Churches of Christ in the United States
of America. Used by permission. All rights reserved.

Cover illustration: *Well Spring* © Jenny Meehan; All Rights Reserved, DACS 2015

A catalogue record for this book is available from the British Library

Printed and bound by CPI Group (UK) Ltd, Croydon CR0 4YY

# The Recovery
## of Hope

### Bible reflections

for sensing God's presence
& hearing God's call

Naomi Starkey

*To all who know they need hope—*
*perhaps this book can offer a signpost or two for the journey.*

## Acknowledgements

Thanks to my colleagues clerical and editorial for help
in shaping this book, especially Andy for suggesting
the title and Lisa for being my right-hand woman
over so many years.

# Contents

# Introduction

As a 'cradle Christian', I cannot recall a time when I did not believe the truths of the faith, when Sunday worship was not as much part of life's routine as eating and sleeping. But (as many much wiser people have reflected and written) I came to realise that there is always more to know of God. There is always more that he wants to do in and through us. While the gospel can be summarised in a few words (try John 3:16, for example), the implications of those few words may well take all eternity for us fully to comprehend.

This book brings together a selection of Bible readings that I originally wrote for *New Daylight* during my years as its editor. As I reviewed my contributions, I found that I had been drawn to a recognisable pattern of themes that related to my own pilgrimage of faith: the hunger for God's consoling presence especially during hard times, the challenge to respond to his call on my life, and the discovery (and rediscovery, again and again) of the deep reassurance that I am not only known but loved beyond understanding.

So I have woven these readings into a kind of journey towards the recovery of hope, the hope of experiencing first-hand the utter sufficiency of God's grace and love and forgiveness, a hope that we may know with our heads a while—perhaps even a long while—before we truly feel it in our hearts. It is the hope of knowing God not only as consoling presence in the darkness but in the challenge of responding to his call and in the transformative experience of knowing how much we are his beloved children.

I have added some poems that I have written along the way, expressing some of the same thoughts and emotions in slightly different terms.

# Words of knowledge

Sometimes
God speaks in neon signs,
Slogans branding public buildings,
Text message straight to the heart.

'Everything will be all right'
I guess so...
Though I can't
For the very life of me
Imagine how.

'Take courage'
OK...
I will take enough for today
And hope there will be some left over
For tomorrow.

'Wait in the unknowing'
I'll try...
Still anxiously reconfiguring
The feasible options
'Until the unknowing is known'.

'There is nothing for you in the desert'
Oh...
But I'd thought this was where I should stay,
Balancing the burden
For the effort of the next step.

And with that,
A glimpse of different possibilities,
A smoother path under clearing skies,
The recovery—
So gentle a surprise—
Of hope.

# — Part 1 —

# Coping with darkness

To begin the journey towards recovering hope, we must first of all find our feet and gather enough strength to start walking, even if we have little idea of where we should be heading. Doing that, strangely enough, may well involve coming to terms with the dark place where we currently find ourselves. We have to know our starting point, avoid panicking over the fear that we can't deal with it, and take a deep breath—and then another. And another. And keep on breathing. Sometimes that is all we can manage; sometimes that is enough.

The following Bible readings cover different aspects of coping with darkness, of living through hard times. Such comfort as they offer is in the context of harsh realities, painful injustice and bitter loss. We hear confidence expressed that God will work out his good purposes, but, until then, the darkness must simply be endured. Life does not go according to our best-laid plans; the in-between, uncomfortable times can feel interminable; we are stuck in Holy Saturday (or even Good Friday), with the joy of Easter tantalisingly beyond reach.

Yet there is that wonderful phrase found in Isaiah 45:3, 'the treasures of darkness'. As we wait, coping in the dark, trusting that things will change but with no idea when, we can still know that God is with us, even if we cannot sense his presence. As the following poem describes, our lives may feel as if we are stumbling along, lonely and aching, but that is not the end of the story. Love—and resurrection joy—have the final word.

# Walking/Wounded

It doesn't feel like courage.
It feels like stumbling,
Falling,
Because the road is rough.
It feels like getting up again
And walking on
When everything feels
Broken.
It feels like choice
That is no choice
But tough, cold necessity.

It may not feel like courage
But others see more clearly—
See strength of will,
Tenacity of soul
And stubborn self-resolve
To carry on in hope,
Because the road dips
Out of sight
And, however far ahead it lies,
At the end
Waits
Love.

# Introduction
## Praying with Psalm 37

Why do bad things happen to good people? Why don't more bad things happen to bad people? These are the dilemmas at the heart of Psalm 37, part of a group of psalms (34—37) that have as their focus godliness and, by contrast, the fate of the wicked. It is generally acceptable to ask why the innocent suffer, but we are probably less comfortable dwelling on why wrongdoers don't get what they deserve when they deserve it. If we have been Christians for any length of time, we know that, like Jesus, we should love and pray for 'sinners'. The psalmists' talk of the 'righteous' may have uncomfortable overtones of self-righteousness to our ears.

While the modern trend is to say that wrongdoing is due to individuals being misunderstood or damaged in some way, the bracing attitude of the Bible is that we all have a choice—as we have had since the very beginning. The consequences of Adam and Eve's choice in Eden show that, given the ability to choose between good and evil, the human tendency is to go for evil in its various manifestations every time, from Cain murdering his brother in a jealous rage (why couldn't they have just had a fight and then made up?) to the marvel that is the worldwide web being used for the promotion of global terrorism, pornography and endless business scams.

One of the consolations promised to the godly in Psalm 37, and elsewhere, is that they will 'inherit the land', as first promised to Abraham (Genesis 12:1). This psalm is ascribed to David and so predates the catastrophe of the exile, whereby the nation lost the land, being led into captivity for repeatedly failing to keep the terms of God's covenant and choosing evil instead of good. Astonishingly, despite everything, he is willing to forgive them and eventually a remnant return home. The wicked and the righteous receive their just reward, but the outcome is always tempered by God's outrageous mercy.

The question still haunts us, though: why don't wrongdoers get what they deserve? Praying with this psalm lets us voice thoughts and emotions that we may consider too 'unChristian' to express except in the privacy of our hearts. Using the psalmist's words, we can bring ourselves, just as we are, into God's presence. We can tell him what we are thinking and feeling and then wait for his loving and healing response.

# Fret not

Do not fret because of the wicked; do not be envious of wrongdoers; for they will soon fade like the grass, and wither like the green herb. Trust in the Lord, and do good; so you will live in the land, and enjoy security. Take delight in the Lord, and he will give you the desires of your heart. (Psalm 37:1–4)

While we may not go around openly complaining about 'the wicked', how many of us have not at some point looked with envy at somebody who has built a prosperous and successful life on the basis of values that we consider highly dubious? We may have worked hard over many years, been polite to our supervisors, reliable at all times—and then we see a colleague promoted over our heads whom we know to be disloyal and unkind, yet, apparently, their 'face fits', which is considered more important. We may go home and complain angrily to anybody who'll listen, 'It's not fair! Let's all trample on everybody else, because that's clearly the way to get on!'

The psalmist, though, tells us not to 'fret' (a wonderful word), because 'the wicked' are as transient as grass. 'That's all very well,' we may respond, 'but they still seem to be flourishing nicely. Exactly when will they start withering?' This is the challenge: we have to trust that God's way is the best way, even if we feel as if we are waiting endlessly for the benefits to come through.

What we are called to do is 'live in the land' where we can enjoy 'security'. Ours is to be long-term, rooted and sustainable growth, a bit like the difference between flowers that pop up in the local park and look lovely for a week or two and trees that mature over decades until they are big enough to endure conditions that would wipe out those showy but transient blooms. The final verse here brings a wonderful promise: if we 'delight' (the Hebrew word implies intense pleasure, not just a hesitant 'Er, that's nice' response) in the Lord, he will give us what we most long for.

— Reflection —

*What is your heart's desire?*
*Bring it to God and await his response.*

# I'm telling you again—fret not

Commit your way to the Lord; trust in him, and he will act. He will make your vindication shine like the light, and the justice of your cause like the noonday. Be still before the Lord, and wait patiently for him; do not fret over those who prosper in their way, over those who carry out evil devices. Refrain from anger, and forsake wrath. Do not fret—it leads only to evil. For the wicked shall be cut off, but those who wait for the Lord shall inherit the land. Yet a little while, and the wicked will be no more; though you look diligently for their place, they will not be there. But the meek shall inherit the land, and delight themselves in abundant prosperity. (Psalm 37:5–11)

In case we hadn't got the message, the psalmist tells us again (and again): don't fret. Instead of agonising about our circumstances, wringing our hands over whether we have made the right decisions or not and even mentally stamping our feet and shouting for God to do something, we are to be patient and 'still before the Lord'.

In Psalm 46:10 we find a better-known verse, one that has inspired many songs of worship: 'Be still, and know that I am God'. In Psalm 37, though, the context is less praise to the Lord, more robust advice for his people. If we decide that patience is a second-best approach to life, we should heed the warning that anger and impatience can actually lead to 'evil'. Frustration is an ugly, fast-growing weed (I'm thinking Japanese knotweed) that, if we are not careful, can grow until it smothers any trace of peace and joy.

As well as 'inheriting the land' (a promise resonating with Jesus' 'Blessed are the meek, for they will inherit the earth', Matthew 5:5), those who wait patiently are promised 'abundant prosperity'. Such words may not particularly stir our hearts, but we should remember that, wherever we are on the globe, we are only a plane-ride away from places where 'peace and prosperity' remain a distant dream. This is a promise to treasure.

— Prayer —

*Lord God, we release into your loving hands our frustration and impatience; grant us a measure of your infinite patience.*

# The baddies' come-uppance

The wicked plot against the righteous, and gnash their teeth at them; but the Lord laughs at the wicked, for he sees that their day is coming. The wicked draw the sword and bend their bows to bring down the poor and needy, to kill those who walk uprightly; their sword shall enter their own heart, and their bows shall be broken. Better is a little that the righteous person has than the abundance of many wicked. For the arms of the wicked shall be broken, but the Lord upholds the righteous. (Psalm 37:12–17)

The picture painted in these verses is a classic cartoon moment: the bad guy picks up an enormous hammer to crush the little guy and manages to hit himself on the head. He plants one of those fizzing fuse bombs, which explodes and leaves him blinking in a smear of soot. Watching events unfold is the Lord, laughing at the stupidity of those who think they can destroy those whom he holds close to his heart.

In parts of scripture we find the assurance that the righteous will be blessed with material prosperity, so it is very interesting to find righteousness equated with poverty here. That is why a 'proof-texting' approach to the Bible can lead to such a plethora of dodgy ideas. What one passage says has to be held in tension with the different perspectives found elsewhere. This psalm describes a context in which being good has to be its own reward, at least for now. Everybody else is 'on the make' and doing extremely well—for now. That, though, is not how the story will end.

Whereas the previous reading warned of the need for patience, this is a call to contentment. We must be content with what we have, even if it is less than we feel we deserve, because we have a wider perspective. As Jesus pointed out (Matthew 6:19–21), we can store 'treasures in heaven', with the promise, a few verses later (v. 33), that, if we seek to live by the values of God's kingdom, we will find that our earthly needs (remembering that they are not the same as wants) are supplied as well.

— Prayer —

*Lord God, we release into your loving hands our neediness;*
*grant us your peace that passes understanding.*

# Vanishing in a puff of smoke

The Lord knows the days of the blameless, and their heritage
will abide for ever; they are not put to shame in evil times,
in the days of famine they have abundance. But the wicked
perish, and the enemies of the Lord are like the glory of the
pastures; they vanish—like smoke they vanish away. The
wicked borrow, and do not pay back, but the righteous are
generous and keep giving; for those blessed by the Lord shall
inherit the land, but those cursed by him shall be cut off.
(Psalm 37:18–22)

The promised blessings here sound reckless in their generosity.
Abundance in times of famine? How could this happen in an
era before NGOs, charity media campaigns and government
aid programmes? Even a cursory reading of Leviticus and
Deuteronomy, though, confirms that God's laws were
designed to create a community where all had enough and
the poor and needy were cared for, even when times were
hard. The actions of Joseph in Egypt (Genesis 41:41–57) also
show that food aid programmes are no modern invention.

The blessings of God's kingdom are released when the
values of his kingdom permeate a community and the
individuals within it. In a society characterised by mistrust
and corruption, nobody sees the point of investing in the
'common life'—and that is why God's people are called to be
'salt and light' (another link to the Sermon on the Mount).
It is easy to assume that any kind of God-given 'call' must
be to full-time church ministry or being a mission worker
somewhere very hot and daunting, but is it not also possible

that we may be called to work for God, embodying the values of God, in business, government or the public sector?

We also find here the troubling idea of the Lord's 'curse', the wicked 'going up in smoke'. It is troubling to think of God being anything other than love, yet within scripture we find promises of mercy and forgiveness as well as stern warnings about the consequences of sinful, rebellious behaviour. If we choose to go our own way, we will be allowed to do so, though the outcomes will be very different.

— Prayer and reflection —

*Pray for your local government councillors—and consider whether God might be calling you or somebody you know to serve him in that context.*

# Reciprocal generosity

Our steps are made firm by the Lord, when he delights in our way; though we stumble, we shall not fall headlong, for the Lord holds us by the hand. I have been young, and now am old, yet I have not seen the righteous forsaken or their children begging bread. They are ever giving liberally and lending, and their children become a blessing. (Psalm 37:23–26)

We only have to browse internet news sites or newspapers to be taken aback by the forthright confidence expressed in these verses. It is all too easy to find examples of countries where devout Christians and their families are starving and suffering. This psalm is identified as being 'of David', so are we supposed to take this as literally suggesting that no good people ever went hungry in his lifetime in ancient Israel—or is it poetic licence? I think the key to the point being made lies in the final sentence: the righteous are not forsaken—and they are characterised as being 'always generous' (v. 26, NIV).

Let me explain: as we reflected in our previous reading, when a society becomes characterised by godly virtues such as kindness, patience, love and generosity, then everyone benefits, whatever their material status. In this, we can detect a foreshadowing of Jesus' words, 'Ask, and it will be given to you; search, and you will find; knock, and the door will be opened for you' (Matthew 7:7). We tend to read this verse from the Sermon on the Mount as relating to persistence in prayer, but imagine the impact if such a pattern of mutual giving and receiving characterised the everyday life of a community or even a whole country!

I read an analysis of American concerns about government health care reforms which argued that resistance to national initiatives sprang in part from a desire to return to the days when charitable works arose naturally from the neighbourly impulses of small-town life, as opposed to 'welfare' imposed by an impersonal system of taxation and legal decree. The extent to which that idyllic 'old-time' scenario was ever realised is debatable, but the principle involved remains a challenging one.

## — Reflection —

*Supporting fair trade initiatives is an excellent way to play a part in the building of global systems that provide mutual benefit. Is yours a fair trade church?*

# People of the land

Depart from evil, and do good; so you shall abide for ever. For the Lord loves justice; he will not forsake his faithful ones. The righteous shall be kept safe for ever, but the children of the wicked shall be cut off. The righteous shall inherit the land, and live in it for ever. The mouths of the righteous utter wisdom, and their tongues speak justice. The law of their God is in their hearts; their steps do not slip. The wicked watch for the righteous, and seek to kill them. The Lord will not abandon them to their power, or let them be condemned when they are brought to trial. (Psalm 37:27–33)

We now reflect a bit further on the central promise of this psalm, that the righteous will 'inherit the land'. The 'land' means the promised land, the land of Israel, the precise borders of which were not made entirely clear, although a commonly used term was 'from Dan to Beersheba' (1 Samuel 3:20; 1 Kings 4:25; 2 Chronicles 30:5). 'The Land', *Haaretz* in Hebrew, is today the name of Israel's oldest daily newspaper (founded in 1918 while the British ruled what was then Palestine).

To us, the idea of 'inheriting the land' may have overtones of being 'landed gentry'. If we own land, we have power over it and even over any people who may live on it, although that power is limited by law. I recall, not so many years ago, speaking to a woman who still remembered her father's fear of losing his tied cottage if the lord of the manor did not see him in church on Sundays.

All talk of 'the land' in the Old Testament, though, was

balanced by the astonishing terms of the Year of Jubilee (Leviticus 25:8–55). Every 50 years, all land was to be returned to its original owners, so nobody amassed property and passed it down through their family for ever. Thus, the righteous will inherit the land but remain tenants of the Lord, who, if they are faithful to his covenant with them, will be the most benevolent of landlords.

## — Reflection —

*'If you follow my statutes and keep my commandments and observe them faithfully… I will walk among you, and will be your God, and you shall be my people' (Leviticus 26:3, 12).*

# The Lord our stronghold

Wait for the Lord, and keep to his way, and he will exalt you to inherit the land; you will look on the destruction of the wicked. I have seen the wicked oppressing, and towering like a cedar of Lebanon. Again I passed by, and they were no more; though I sought them, they could not be found. Mark the blameless, and behold the upright, for there is posterity for the peaceable. But transgressors shall be altogether destroyed; the posterity of the wicked shall be cut off. The salvation of the righteous is from the Lord; he is their refuge in the time of trouble. The Lord helps them and rescues them; he rescues them from the wicked, and saves them, because they take refuge in him. (Psalm 37:34–40)

It is interesting to see how the imagery develops in this psalm. In the opening verses, the wicked are like grass and green plants, lush but transient. Later on, they are compared to meadow flowers but now they are said to flourish 'like a cedar of Lebanon'. Hang on, isn't such strength and vigour supposed to be the preserve of God's favoured ones, who (according to Isaiah 61:3) 'will be called oaks of righteousness, the planting of the Lord, to display his glory'? The ruthless people here are not only still growing; they now look like a deeply rooted and traditional part of the landscape, protected by tree preservation orders.

Leaping to the very end of the Bible, we find the evil forces opposing God portrayed in terrifying imagery of dragons, giant insects, horned sea-monsters and an army so vast that they are like the sand on the seashore (Revelation 20:8). The book of Revelation does not spare us the horror—but nor does it diminish the scale of the victory, already won, of light over darkness.

However unchecked and pervasive the might of the wicked, however apparently hopeless the plight of the righteous, there is always the firm hope of deliverance. For the psalmist, that deliverance comes through the Lord, our 'stronghold in times of trouble'; for the writer of Revelation, there is the assurance of the almighty power on the throne of heaven and the risen Lamb of God.

— Prayer —

*Almighty Father, you are our strong tower. We shelter in you and know that in you we can hope for deliverance.*

# Introduction
## 2 Kings 13—17

It is probably safe to say that the latter chapters of 2 Kings are among the less well-known in the Bible. The colourful characters have gone—no more Solomons, Elijahs or Jezebels—and what we find is an apparently unending series of calamitous monarchs, set on leading their people to disaster. Our section (chapters 13—17) begins with bad King Jehoahaz of Israel and concludes with the downfall of what had been his kingdom at the hands of the Assyrians.

What can we learn from this litany of trouble, struggle and eventual catastrophe? In the Hebrew Bible (what Christians call the Old Testament), 1 and 2 Kings are the last of the former prophets (Joshua, Judges, Samuel, Kings) and these books present a particular—prophetic—view of history. They are prophetic in the sense not of foretelling the future but of laying bare the spiritual reality of a situation, the divine perspective on human affairs. In the stories of the books of Kings, the same pattern recurs: the people are disobedient; they suffer (often as a result of foreign invasion); they cry out to God, who rescues them; national life is restored to peace and prosperity; the people are disobedient again. From a human perspective, the events may have seemed a haphazard sequence of troubles; from God's perspective, there was a clear chain of cause and effect.

Nowadays, we tend to judge governments primarily on how they handle the economy, but, when passing judgement on kings such as Jehoahaz, Amaziah, Azariah and Pekah, what mattered to the writers of Kings were their religious policies—whether they encouraged the worship of other gods or tolerated worship of the true God conducted outside Jerusalem. We only discover anything about contemporary social conditions via comments in other prophetic writings of the time. Imagine a history of modern-day Britain written from such a standpoint!

As we read these passages, we must engage our imaginations to discern something of the human suffering behind the stark narrative. We must also open our hearts to learning more of the nature of God and his working in history, despite the grim nature of so many of those stories.

# Anger and mercy

Jehoahaz son of Jehu began to reign over Israel... The anger of the Lord was kindled against Israel, so that he gave them repeatedly into the hand of King Hazael of Aram, then into the hand of Ben-hadad son of Hazael. But Jehoahaz entreated the Lord, and the Lord heeded him; for he saw the oppression of Israel, how the king of Aram oppressed them. Therefore the Lord gave Israel a saviour, so that they escaped from the hand of the Arameans; and the people of Israel lived in their homes as formerly. Nevertheless, they did not depart from the sins of the house of Jeroboam. (2 Kings 13:1, 3–6, abridged)

In this passage, we see played out the chain of events outlined in the Introduction to these notes: disobedience (verse 2 tells how the king's sins led his entire people astray), disaster, pleas for mercy, salvation, restoration—and continued disobedience.

The phrase 'the anger of the Lord' may trouble us, because we are used to thinking that our God is a God of love. We may be disturbed by ideas of an 'angry Old Testament God', but the same Old Testament also tells us that God's anger is slow to kindle (Exodus 34:6–7). Further, today's story demonstrates divine mercy and pity just as much as anger. After all, Israel had been warned about keeping its side of God's covenant, with the dire consequences spelled out by prophet after prophet. Here, though, the very same king who 'did what was evil in the sight of the Lord' (2 Kings 13:2) entreats the Lord for deliverance—and, astonishingly, an unidentified 'saviour' is sent (v. 5). The people escape, then settle back home with sighs of relief. Nothing changes.

Reflecting on our own lives, we may be aware of times when God has acted to save us, perhaps even before we were aware that we needed saving. When we identify such times, are we open to learning whatever lessons he would have us learn?

## — Reflection —

*'Jerusalem… the city that kills the prophets and stones those who are sent to it! How often have I desired to gather your children together as a hen gathers her brood under her wings, and you were not willing!' (Luke 13:34).*

# The benefit of hindsight

In the thirty-seventh year of King Joash of Judah, Jehoash son
of Jehoahaz began to reign over Israel… Now when Elisha had
fallen sick with the illness of which he was to die, King Joash
of Israel went down to him, and wept before him, crying, 'My
father, my father! The chariots of Israel and its horsemen!'
Elisha said to him, '… The Lord's arrow of victory, the arrow of
victory over Aram! For you shall fight the Arameans in Aphek
until you have made an end of them'… So Elisha died, and
they buried him. (2 Kings 13:10, 14–17, 20, abridged)

Here we say goodbye to Elisha, one of the last major Old
Testament 'characters' whose personalities loom as large as
their messages. The strange words that the king weeps over
the dying man are the same as Elisha himself cried out as his
'father in God', Elijah, disappeared from view (2 Kings 2:12).
Commentators are unsure whether they imply 'heavenly
hosts' coming to collect the prophet or that the prophet was
a strong defender of Israel. Either way, they reverberate with
grief and loss.

In every generation, God gifts certain people with
unusual powers of insight into the affairs of the world and
the motivations of the human heart. Few would be happy
to claim the title 'prophet' for themselves, and rightly so,
yet they undeniably have prophetic gifts. Their task is, as
it has always been, to challenge the status quo, question
assumptions and call the church to account—and they often
get a hostile reception. Nobody likes their certainties shaken,

especially those who are certain that their beliefs represent the only possible truth.

With hindsight, the God-given quality of these prophetic words may be recognised, even as their immediate challenge is diminished by the passage of time. The Israelite king in our passage (also known as Joash, confusingly) is recorded as having done 'evil in the sight of the Lord' (13:11). Is his grief as much for his own stubbornness in not heeding the prophet in his lifetime as for Elisha's imminent demise?

— Reflection —

*Hindsight is a wonderful thing, but it is better to pray for courage here and now to acknowledge whatever prophetic insights may be presented to us.*

# Limits on chaos

In the second year of King Joash... of Israel, King Amaziah son of Joash of Judah began to reign... He did what was right in the sight of the Lord, yet not like his ancestor David; in all things he did as his father Joash had done. But the high places were not removed; the people still sacrificed and made offerings on the high places. As soon as the royal power was firmly in his hand he killed his servants who had murdered his father the king. But he did not put to death the children of the murderers. (2 Kings 14:1, 3–6, abridged)

Here is a little relief in the catalogue of woeful rulers—but only a little. Amaziah of Judah 'did what was right', but he was not considered as good as David, the gold standard for kingship. In line with the agenda of the writers (identified by scholars as the 'Deuteronomistic historians', because their perspective is also evident in Deuteronomy), Amaziah's limitations are evident in the fact that he does not remove the 'high places'—unofficial altars used for worship rituals outside Jerusalem—and restrict worship to the temple.

Bizarrely, to our ears, he is cited as acting 'according to what is written in the book of the law of Moses' (v. 6) because he murders only the servants who killed his father and not their children. Is this yet another example of a horrible 'Old Testament God' advocating violence or, rather, should we note the fact that God's law limited retribution, in contrast to traditions that prevailed over many centuries in many imperial systems around the world?

It is interesting to reflect on the broad sweep of God's law in the light of Jesus' remark: 'Because of your hardness of heart he wrote this commandment for you' (Mark 10:5). The context for that remark was a challenge about divorce, but the point surely is that God's law so often provides for—or restricts—the chaos created by human sinfulness. In the world as God originally intended (and, as we are promised, it will be again one day), such sinfulness will no longer have the power to mar relationships, whether between individuals or across society.

— Reflection —

*O Lord, have mercy on us, miserable offenders…*

# Battle bravado

Then Amaziah sent messengers to King Jehoash… of Israel, saying, 'Come, let us look one another in the face.' King Jehoash of Israel sent word to King Amaziah of Judah, '… You have indeed defeated Edom, and your heart has lifted you up. Be content with your glory, and stay at home; for why should you provoke trouble so that you fall, you and Judah with you?' But Amaziah would not listen. So King Jehoash of Israel went up; he and King Amaziah of Judah faced one another in battle… Judah was defeated by Israel; everyone fled home. (2 Kings 14:8–12, abridged)

This story (do take a moment to read it in full in your own Bible) has a troubling air of playground swagger about it: 'I dare you… come and take me on—if you're hard enough!' Amaziah of Judah had already soundly defeated the Edomites (v. 7), but, as Jehoash (or Joash) of Israel points out, he seems to want to provoke trouble. What follows is catastrophic for Judah. The 'alpha males' face up to one another on the battlefield. They fight—Israel against Judah, cousin against cousin—and the kingdom of Judah and the city of Jerusalem are left broken and plundered.

Now, what was the point of that, boys?

So often, wars are later judged to have been waged for selfish or simply stupid motives. While rhetoric at the time may glorify a planned conflict, the cost in human suffering (whether intentional or 'collateral damage') is terrible. Some situations seem to argue for warfare as the lesser of two evils, but we should not forget that admitting such an argument still names war as evil. It is not good, not as God intended the world to be. Reading of war between Israel and Judah is particularly poignant in the light of how God's people were intended to live. God had warned, through the prophet Samuel, that becoming a monarchy would not improve the nation (1 Samuel 8); today's story reads like the sad coda to that warning. They got a king and what followed was conflict upon conflict.

— Prayer —

*Lord God, we pray for your blessing and protection on all those who work for peace. Grace them with courage and perseverance in their task.*

# Saved by a bad king

> In the fifteenth year of King Amaziah... King Jeroboam son
> of Joash of Israel began to reign in Samaria... He restored the
> border of Israel... according to the word of the Lord, the God
> of Israel, which he spoke by his servant Jonah son of Amittai,
> the prophet, who was from Gath-hepher. For the Lord saw
> that the distress of Israel was very bitter; there was no one
> left, bond or free, and no one to help Israel. But the Lord had
> not said that he would blot out the name of Israel from under
> heaven, so he saved them by the hand of Jeroboam son of
> Joash. (2 Kings 14:23, 25–27, abridged)

In a single verse, another famous Old Testament character
makes a fleeting appearance. This is the only reference to the
prophet Jonah outside his own book, with scholars making
a case for the story of his trip to Nineveh being written later
than 1 and 2 Kings, to teach specific lessons about God's
mercy. Even so, it is intriguing to find this tiny snapshot of
Jonah engaged in the prophetic task closer to home.

The prophets Amos and Hosea were contemporaries of
Jeroboam and a glance at their books reveals something of
the social and moral conditions of the times. Theirs was an
economically divided society, the wealthy enjoying leisured
luxury while the poor worked for a pittance. Does that ring
any disturbingly contemporary bells?

Jeroboam of Israel (who is actually Jeroboam II, Jeroboam
I having been the first ruler of Israel after the split with
Judah: 1 Kings 12:20) is not cited as being a good king ('he
did what was evil', 2 Kings 14:24). Despite this, God uses him

to deliver Israel from their 'bitter distress'. Just because we find God's blessing on our enterprise, we should not assume that all we do, think and say enjoys the same blessing. The purposes of God are beyond our comprehension; if we sense our part in the unfolding of those purposes, our response should be humility and gratitude. We should never permit ourselves any arrogant 'God is on our side' assumptions.

## — Reflection —

*'So if you think you are standing, watch out that you do not fall' (1 Corinthians 10:12).*

# Anarchy rules

Shallum son of Jabesh began to reign in the thirty-ninth year of King Uzziah of Judah; he reigned one month in Samaria. Then Menahem son of Gadi came up from Tirzah and came to Samaria; he struck down Shallum son of Jabesh in Samaria and killed him; he reigned in place of him. Now the rest of the deeds of Shallum, including the conspiracy that he made, are written in the Book of the Annals of the Kings of Israel. At that time Menahem sacked Tiphsah, all who were in it and its territory from Tirzah on; because they did not open it to him, he sacked it. (2 Kings 15:13–16)

We keep our focus on the kings of Israel here. Over in Jerusalem, (relatively) good King Amaziah of Judah has been murdered after a conspiracy (14:19), succeeded by his son Azariah (also known as Uzziah, 15:13; see Isaiah 6:1). He reigned for 52 years, during which time the Samaria-based Israelite throne changed hands five times.

King Shallum is violently overthrown, just as he violently overthrew the previous king, Zechariah son of Jeroboam II, who had reigned for just six months (2 Kings 15:8–10). Shallum's reign has an even briefer span—a single month—and Menahem, the brutal warlord who succeeds him, has a record of such atrocity that I could not bear to include the final part of verse 16 in today's reading. Like a virus, violence rages across the lands. The only true king now is Anarchy.

Thanks to the worldwide web of communications, we have no excuse for ignorance: there are still far too many parts of the world where the rule of law is non-existent, where might is always right, where the loudest, harshest voices drown out all else. God's command to his people was, 'You shall love your neighbour as yourself' (Leviticus 19:18). If 'neighbours' are those with whom we can be in daily contact, then these days we cannot plead geographical distance in mitigation of our lack of love and care for the most vulnerable in our world.

## — Prayer —

*Lord God, give us compassionate hearts—and eyes to see where and how you call us to show that compassion.*

# Desperate times

In the thirty-ninth year of King Azariah of Judah, Menahem son of Gadi began to reign over Israel; he reigned for ten years in Samaria. He did what was evil in the sight of the Lord... King Pul of Assyria came against the land; Menahem gave Pul a thousand talents of silver, so that he might help him confirm his hold on the royal power. Menahem exacted the money from Israel, that is, from all the wealthy, fifty shekels of silver from each one, to give to the king of Assyria. So the king of Assyria turned back, and did not stay there in the land. (2 Kings 15:17–20, abridged)

We are nearing the end of the northern kingdom. The menace of Assyria appears over the horizon and the nation that once relied on the Lord God to save them from their enemies is reduced to begging for piles of silver to pay off the aggressive foreign power. We can get some idea of the amount of silver involved by the fact that a single talent weighed around 33 kg.

It can be disconcerting to realise how relatively insignificant both Israel and Judah were in the wider context of the ancient Near East. Israel's situation was desperate: it was a tiny monarchy facing the might of Pul, also known as Tiglath-Pileser III, who ruled as king of both Assyria and Babylon. Visitors to the British Museum in London can look at his likeness in stone—a military conqueror, administrative reformer, imperial potentate. By contrast, being God's people did not involve becoming any kind of superpower.

Working to extend God's kingdom on earth does not, and

never should, result in empire-building. As Jesus taught his followers, and as Paul underlined to the new Christians in Corinth, God's power is all about servanthood, weakness and suffering. When we forget that, and when we act as if it is all about our own strength, influence and power, things will inevitably, eventually, start to go wrong.

## — Reflection —

*'So, I will boast all the more gladly of my weaknesses, so that the power of Christ may dwell in me. Therefore I am content with weaknesses, insults, hardships, persecutions, and calamities for the sake of Christ; for whenever I am weak, then I am strong' (2 Corinthians 12:9–10).*

# Into exile

In the fifty-second year of King Azariah of Judah, Pekah son of Remaliah began to reign over Israel in Samaria; he reigned for twenty years… King Tiglath-pileser of Assyria came and captured Ijon, Abel-beth-maacah, Janoah, Kedesh, Hazor, Gilead, and Galilee, all the land of Naphtali; and he carried the people captive to Assyria. Then Hoshea son of Elah made a conspiracy against Pekah son of Remaliah, attacked him, and killed him; he reigned in place of him, in the twentieth year of Jotham son of Uzziah. (2 Kings 15:27, 29–30)

The throne of Israel changes hands for the fifth time, while King Azariah/Uzziah is still on the throne of Judah. The new Israelite king is Pekah, son of royal military captain Remaliah, who wrests power from Pekahiah, the son of Menahem, after a mere two-year reign. Pekah himself manages 20 years, but they are hardly a triumph. Not only does he do 'evil' in God's sight (v. 28) but Menahem's policy of paying off Assyria is shown to have failed spectacularly. Tiglath-Pileser returns, captures a string of settlements and territory and deports the people to Assyria. The descendants of the people rescued from slavery in the exodus are now forcibly removed and taken on a new journey into captivity—the exile. Presumably in response to such disaster, Pekah is overthrown and murdered by Hoshea, who turns out to be the very last king of Israel.

Tales of Assyrian brutality are, some say, exaggerated, but even setting aside deliberate acts of torture and humiliation, the trauma of deportation should not be underestimated. Resettling entire populations was a feature of Stalinist policy during and after World War II, resulting in countless deaths. Critics of Christianity will hold up examples of wickedness perpetrated in the name of the church, such as the Crusades and the Spanish Inquisition. What is sadly clear from even the briefest survey of history is that humanity's capacity for cruelty seems limitless.

## — Reflection —

*It is the work of 21st-century prophetic preachers… to name the despair and to witness to the divine resolve for newness that may break the vicious cycles of self-destruction and make new common life possible.*

Walter Brueggemann, *The Practice of Prophetic Imagination* (Fortress, 2012)

# A very bad king

In the seventeenth year of Pekah son of Remaliah, King Ahaz son of Jotham of Judah began to reign… He did not do what was right in the sight of the Lord his God, as his ancestor David had done, but he walked in the way of the kings of Israel. He even made his son pass through fire, according to the abominable practices of the nations whom the Lord drove out before the people of Israel. He sacrificed and made offerings on the high places, on the hills, and under every green tree. (2 Kings 16:1–4, abridged)

Time now for a catch-up on what had been happening in the southern kingdom of Judah. King Azariah/Uzziah finally died, two years after his Golden Jubilee, although, as he was suffering from leprosy (15:5), his son Jotham took charge in the final stages of his reign. Like his father, Jotham was judged as having done 'right in the eyes of the Lord' but still was not determined enough to rid the country of the old worship sites (15:34–35). Compared with its northern neighbour, Judah seemed to have at least some stability and at least adequate leadership, but then the throne passed to Ahaz.

Note that this is 'Ahaz', not 'Ahab' of Israel, who appears in 1 Kings and tussles with Elijah. Ahaz of Judah not only 'walked in the ways of the kings of Israel' (v. 3)—not a compliment—but also led the further fragmentation of worship and, worse still, even seems to have conducted child sacrifice (a practice also mentioned in 3:27).

Leadership, whether of an organisation, community,

church or nation, does so much to set the tone for the lives of the people who are, in many ways, in that leadership's care. In a country where getting to the top means being able to drain the economy to fill your and your family's bank accounts, for example, honesty is hardly commended to the wider population. Power is a dangerous, potentially toxic brew—and unlimited power should mean unlimited responsibility, not unlimited venality.

— Prayer —

*Lord God, grant grace and honesty to our governments and wise insight to all with the charisma of leadership.*

# Your servant and your son

Then King Rezin of Aram and King Pekah son of Remaliah of Israel came up to wage war on Jerusalem; they besieged Ahaz but could not conquer him. At that time the king of Edom recovered Elath for Edom, and drove the Judeans from Elath… Ahaz sent messengers to King Tiglath-pileser of Assyria, saying, 'I am your servant and your son. Come up and rescue me…' Ahaz also took the silver and gold found in the house of the Lord and in the treasures of the king's house, and sent a present to the king of Assyria. The king of Assyria listened to him; the king of Assyria marched up against Damascus, and took it, carrying its people captive to Kir. (2 Kings 16:5–9, abridged)

'Aram' is another name for Syria (the capital of which, Damascus, is recorded here as being conquered). Syria and Israel had joined in an unsuccessful attack on Judah, also mentioned in Isaiah 7:1–17 and Hosea 5:8–15, where the prophet warns of the danger of accepting Assyrian help (as well as in 2 Chronicles 28, both books of Chronicles offering their own take on events recounted in 1 and 2 Kings).

Ahaz's words to Tiglath-Pileser read as deeply ironic. Time and again the Old Testament uses the words 'servant' and 'son' to refer to the relationship between the Lord God and his chosen people, but here they are used in grovelling appeal to the Assyrian king, combined with a reckless ransacking of the temple and the king's own treasury, not even selling but giving away the family silver (and gold). Ahaz wins a reprieve for Judah, but only for the short term.

There is no mention of him crying out to the Lord for deliverance as he struggles to shore up the crumbling borders of his kingdom. Sadly, the further we walk from God, the harder we can find it to return, even when we most need to do so. If our wrongful actions unleash chaos, that chaos may well run its course, no matter how fervently we then repent and call for heavenly help.

## — Reflection —

*'See, the Lord's hand is not too short to save, nor his ear too dull to hear. Rather, your iniquities have been barriers between you and your God' (Isaiah 59:1–2).*

# Multitude of sacrifices

The priest Uriah built the altar; in accordance with all that King Ahaz had sent from Damascus... The king drew near to the altar, went up on it, and offered his burnt-offering and his grain-offering, poured his drink-offering, and dashed the blood of his offerings of well-being against the altar... King Ahaz commanded the priest Uriah, saying, 'Upon the great altar offer the morning burnt-offering, and the evening grain-offering, and the king's burnt-offering, and his grain-offering, with the burnt-offering of all the people of the land, their grain-offering, and their drink-offering... but the bronze altar shall be for me to inquire by.' (2 Kings 16:11–13, 15, abridged)

The context for today's passage is King Ahaz's visit to the Assyrian king in Damascus (v. 10), where he decides that the Jerusalem temple must have an identical altar to the one there. Uriah obliges, copying the model sent by Ahaz, who later (vv. 17–18) rearranges and remakes some of the other temple furnishings, 'because of the king of Assyria' (v. 18). Perhaps this work indicates his new, subject status, needing to placate his imperial overlord.

The passage is notable for its details of the routine sacrifices offered by both the king and the people of Judah. The Hebrew phrase for 'offering of well-being' used to be translated 'peace offering'. It involved burning part of the sacrificial animal, giving part to the priests and feasting on the rest. The burnt (animal) and grain offerings were burned entirely.

The king tells Uriah that he will use the old bronze altar to 'inquire by' (v. 15). This probably refers to divination—looking for good and bad omens by examining animal entrails, a practice banned in Deuteronomy 18:10–12, along with making children 'pass through fire', which Ahaz has also done. He seems to be keeping up the sacrificial system but ignoring the bigger problem—that he is far from God, struggling to save himself and his kingdom by his own feeble efforts.

## — Reflection —

*'What to me is the multitude of your sacrifices? … When you stretch out your hands, I will hide my eyes from you; even though you make many prayers, I will not listen; your hands are full of blood' (Isaiah 1:11, 15).*

# The bitter end for Israel

In the twelfth year of King Ahaz of Judah, Hoshea son of Elah began to reign in Samaria... King Shalmaneser of Assyria came up against him; Hoshea became his vassal, and paid him tribute. But the king of Assyria found treachery in Hoshea; for he had sent messengers to King So of Egypt, and offered no tribute to the king of Assyria... therefore the king of Assyria confined him and imprisoned him. Then the king of Assyria invaded all the land and came to Samaria; for three years he besieged it. In the ninth year of Hoshea the king of Assyria captured Samaria; he carried the Israelites away to Assyria. (2 Kings 17:1, 3–6, abridged)

Thus, the end comes. Hoshea has foolishly conspired with Egypt against Shalmaneser (son of Tiglath-Pileser) of Assyria, so he is punished and Samaria besieged. Assyrian inscriptions record that, by the time the three-year siege ended, the Assyrian conqueror was Sargon II, successor to Shalmaneser, and the people of Israel had been deported hundreds of miles, into the heart of their enemy's empire. The books of Nehemiah and Ezra tell how the people of Judah were later permitted to return from their own period of exile, but such permission was never granted to those from Israel. Speculation about the 'lost ten tribes of Israel' continues to this day, with communities across the world claiming to be their descendants (adherents of British Israelism, for example, believing that the British royal family are directly descended from King David).

As a result of the exile, the question reverberating across

the Old Testament is 'How could this happen to God's own people?' What did the exodus and the promised land mean now? A theological reason is provided in tomorrow's passage, but today we have the political/military explanation. Hoshea gambled on an alliance with Egypt and lost, in a reversal of David and Goliath and so many other biblical stories in which victory is won against the odds because of reliance on divine—rather than human—guidance and protection.

— Prayer —

*Lord God, we pray for all those who feel, for whatever reason, exiled and far from home. In your mercy, may they find their home in you.*

# Reasons

> This occurred because the people of Israel had sinned against the Lord their God, who had brought them up out of the land of Egypt from under the hand of Pharaoh king of Egypt. They had worshipped other gods and walked in the customs of the nations whom the Lord drove out before the people of Israel... Judah also did not keep the commandments of the Lord their God but walked in the customs that Israel had introduced. The Lord rejected all the descendants of Israel; he punished them and gave them into the hand of plunderers, until he had banished them from his presence. (2 Kings 17:7–8, 19–20)

The historians of 2 Kings spell out with painful clarity why events unfolded as they did, pointing out that the cause lay in the aftermath of the exodus. Israel chose to follow Canaanite religious practices, offering their worship elsewhere than to the God who had delivered them. Why had no one fully heeded the warnings of the prophets, delivered over so many years? Surely now Judah would learn from the northern kingdom's downfall and choose a better way? The rest of 2 Kings, however, tells the sad tale of the end of the southern kingdom, prefigured here in the judgement that the people persisted in the same wrongful ways as Israel.

We may shake our heads at such folly, but we, too, often persist with our own misguided plans instead of stilling ourselves to tune into God's priorities. We write our own life scripts, scheming for our desired outcomes, then we are shocked if things turn out very differently, perhaps disastrously. The stronger and more capable we think we are, the more tempting it is to believe that our way, our perspective, is the only right way, the only true perspective. We may forget all about listening, waiting, trusting—right up until our circumstances force us to remember.

## — Reflection —

*Prophetic preaching in our time and place fundamentally faces the reality of loss among us that dominant imagination could never, in its wildest imagination, imagine... It is about breaking the code of invulnerability that we had so deeply trusted.*

Walter Brueggemann, *The Practice of Prophetic Imagination* (Fortress, 2012)

# Seeking hope

> The king of Assyria brought people from Babylon… and placed them in the cities of Samaria in place of the people of Israel… When they first settled there, they did not worship the Lord; therefore the Lord sent lions among them, which killed some of them… Then the king of Assyria commanded, 'Send there one of the priests whom you carried away from there; let him go and live there, and teach them the law of the god of the land.' So one of the priests whom they had carried away from Samaria came and lived in Bethel; he taught them how they should worship the Lord. (2 Kings 17:24–25, 27–28, abridged)

Here is the final outworking of the Assyrian imperial policies. Sargon II resettles the more-or-less emptied land of Israel (scholarly opinion differs on the extent of the deportation) with new inhabitants from elsewhere. The land promised to the descendants of Abraham is now given, at least in part, into the hands of others.

This is a challenging episode (setting aside what it means that 'the Lord sent lions' to kill those not practising a religion they had not been taught) because it reminds us that God's agenda is far greater than we understand. His chosen people turned away from him, so they lost their promised land, new people were settled there and they were taught to worship him. Sadly, though, the rest of the chapter explains that the new inhabitants were also unfaithful and disobedient. If we were God, we might have been tempted to give up on the whole human race enterprise, which had generated nothing but grief and bloodshed.

We have already seen in these passages, however, that the kingdom of God is not characterised by the dynamics of empire-building. The hope represented by the promise of God's kingdom is manifest most often at the grassroots of life. No matter how comprehensive the devastation, how strong the sense that the entire ground of our being has been concreted over and rendered sterile, the green shoots of God's life can still break through.

## — Reflection —

*We believe in an eternal, loving God, so there is always hope, even if we struggle to understand what that means in our present circumstances.*

# Introduction
## The absence of God

When we think of 'the absence of God', we probably turn to those times when we have struggled to believe, when 'God' has seemed a distant concept rather than a present and personal reality. An overwhelming sense of God's absence—the 'dark night of the soul', to use a classic spiritual phrase—can be a vivid and painful experience for many. At the same time, it is not beyond the bounds of possibility that sometimes we, and sometimes even our church communities, can end up obscuring rather than enhancing an awareness of God's presence for others.

The following readings are patterned as follows. We shall first take a brief walk through the events of the death, burial and resurrection of Jesus, touching on what they can reveal to us about coping with God's apparent absence. We shall then go on to explore some of the implications, which relate in part to our responsibility as Christians to witness to what we know and believe about God's presence with us, however dark life's circumstances. These implications also point to how we can cling to the fundamental truth that God is indeed with us, 'Emmanuel', no matter how lonely, broken or lost we may feel.

As I have worked through these passages, I have found it fascinating to bring together the idea of God's absence with Ascension—a day in the church's year that can be overlooked in many churches. Might that be because this event is one we struggle to classify? Is it actually an event to celebrate or in some way to mourn? A word that has kept returning to me is 'poignant'—something not easily identifiable as 'happy' or 'sad', but still involving an intensity of emotion that can pierce the heart. The Lord is here, his Spirit is with us—and yet we cannot touch his arm or lean against him, as his friends once touched and leaned. Like them, however, we shall learn to love him with a love that is strong, deep and true, yet is also about releasing to the world, rather than jealously possessing, the Beloved.

# The cry from the cross

My God, my God, why have you forsaken me? Why are you so far from helping me, from the words of my groaning? O my God, I cry by day, but you do not answer; and by night, but find no rest. Yet you are holy, enthroned on the praises of Israel. In you our ancestors trusted; they trusted, and you delivered them. To you they cried, and were saved; in you they trusted, and were not put to shame. But I am a worm, and not human; scorned by others, and despised by the people... But you, O Lord, do not be far away! O my help, come quickly to my aid! (Psalm 22:1–6, 19)

Naked, bloodied, shuddering with cold after three hours of darkness, hanging in torment at the Place of the Skull, Jesus cries out 'with a loud voice' (Mark 15:34) the opening words of this psalm. Dare we paraphrase it as 'screamed'— or does that disturb too much our belief in an omnipotent, omniscient, eternal Saviour?

One of the earliest heresies of the church was docetism, from the Greek *doceo*, 'to seem'. Its proponents contended that Jesus only took on the appearance of humanity, because how could the immortal become mortal? Even today we can struggle to remember the humanity of Christ, forgetting that (as Hebrews 4:15 tells us) he is one 'who in every respect has been tested as we are'.

That cry of Jesus speaks of intense, undeniable humanity. Although he knew he was the Son of God, he could not 'rise above the situation' and 'simply believe', but felt abandoned by the one he called Father. What a comfort that can be to all those who have ever felt guilty for such a response to a difficult situation!

Wonderfully, Psalm 22, like so many other psalms, starts in despair but finishes with words of renewed confidence, even joy. Jesus chose to voice his despair with an ancient prayer that comes, in the end, to affirm that God is good; when we fear we are falling for ever, he is there to catch us.

## — Reflection —

*'He did not hide his face from me, but heard when I cried to him' (Psalm 22:24).*

# Dead and gone

Now there was a good and righteous man named Joseph…
and he was waiting expectantly for the kingdom of God. This
man went to Pilate and asked for the body of Jesus. Then
he took it down, wrapped it in a linen cloth, and laid it in
a rock-hewn tomb where no one had ever been laid… The
women who had come with [Jesus] from Galilee followed,
and they saw the tomb and how his body was laid. Then they
returned, and prepared spices and ointments. On the sabbath
they rested according to the commandment. (Luke 23:50–53,
55–56, abridged)

When somebody is martyred, their dead body has special
significance for their friends and followers—hence the
lengths to which the executioners will go to deny them any
part of that body, and the veneration accorded to 'religious'
relics, such as a single fingerbone, a phial of blood or a lock
of hair. If that makes us feel a bit prickly and Protestant, try
browsing the internet to see how much value can be placed
on 'secular' relics—a signed photograph, a used serviette, a
rock star's unwashed T shirt…

We can only guess at the crushing desolation of Jesus'
disciples on that sabbath eve. If he had been who he had
claimed to be—the Son of God—was God now dead? Were
they facing not only the loss of their master but also the loss
of the faith that had sustained their people for so long? If they
could not bring themselves to believe that, the unavoidable
conclusion was that Jesus had been deluded. Inspirational,

possessed of extraordinary powers, but deluded—and with them no longer.

Matthew tells us (27:55) that the women mentioned here had accompanied Jesus from back home in Galilee to look after him. There seemed nothing left for them to do now except prepare for a final, intimate act of care. Surely many tears were shed as those spices and ointments were prepared—but I imagine that their tears would have arisen from anger and a sense of betrayal as well from love.

— Prayer —

*Thank you, almighty God, that you are bigger than all the anger, pain and loss that we could ever feel. May we remember that and find security in the remembering.*

# Beyond imagining

Mary stood weeping outside the tomb. As she wept, she bent over to look into the tomb; and she saw two angels in white, sitting where the body of Jesus had been lying, one at the head and the other at the feet. They said to her, 'Woman, why are you weeping?' She said to them, 'They have taken away my Lord, and I do not know where they have laid him.' When she had said this, she turned round and saw Jesus standing there, but she did not know that it was Jesus. (John 20:11–14)

In our Easter celebrations, we can overlook the fact that the first resurrection morning began with even bleaker emotions than those that had dominated the previous days. Jesus' body had disappeared. There was nothing left to touch, no focus for mourning, no physical reminder of those brief but breathtaking years of Jesus' ministry.

We may be tempted to rush on to the next verses of the story, when Mary recognises Jesus as he speaks her name. It is poignant, however, to pause at this desolate moment, even as the final sentence of our reading trembles with the glorious miracle to trump all miracles. Maybe Jesus' friends had to face losing their very last reminder of his earthly presence before they could receive what God had in store for them instead—something beyond imagining.

Jesus had a new, resurrection body whereby he was identifiably himself, but not at first glance. He was in some way different, such that even those who knew him struggled to recognise him at first. His familiar and much-loved mortal body was transformed in a foreshadowing of the transformation promised to every child of his Father, every one of us. God's transforming love is at work within our hearts even now, shaping us into the sons and daughters he has always longed for us to be. One day, in his presence, that inner transformation will be fully visible when we, too, are blessed with the healed and heavenly bodies of resurrected life.

— Prayer —

*O God of Easter morning, give us the courage to hold our hands and hearts open to all that you would give us.*

# Stay with us

As [the two disciples] came near the village to which they were going, [Jesus] walked ahead as if he were going on. But they urged him strongly, saying, 'Stay with us, because it is almost evening and the day is now nearly over.' So he went in to stay with them. When he was at the table with them, he took bread, blessed and broke it, and gave it to them. Then their eyes were opened, and they recognised him; and he vanished from their sight. They said to each other, 'Were not our hearts burning within us while he was talking to us on the road, while he was opening the scriptures to us?' (Luke 24:28–32)

I find this one of the most endearing of the resurrection appearances because of its homeliness. Two people are walking sadly home after that terrible Friday in Jerusalem. Jesus comes alongside them, unrecognised, and begins to explain the significance of what has been happening. When they reach their destination, Jesus seems about to walk on into the night, but is persuaded to join them for supper and more conversation. Their new friend prays a blessing on the bread and breaks it—just as he did at the Passover supper before he died—and it is then that they know him, whereupon he vanishes.

There it is again, that note of poignancy. Jesus is alive again, but in a different way. He is there, but then he is not. They cannot hold on to him; they have to accept his presence not as a special favour limited to his closest friends, but as a gift to empower them to share abroad the astonishingly good news of the kingdom.

We may fear that we will never be brave or strong enough to make use of such a gift. Indeed, our present circumstances may speak to us only of divine absence or indifference rather than presence. The story of that encounter on the Emmaus road can give us hope, though, that even if our days feel like a dreary trudge, we do not trudge alone.

— Prayer —

*Risen Jesus, open our eyes to see you walking with us as we continue our journey through the life with which we have been blessed.*

# Returning with great joy

[Jesus] said to [his followers], 'Thus it is written, that the Messiah is to suffer and to rise from the dead on the third day, and that repentance and forgiveness of sins is to be proclaimed in his name to all nations, beginning from Jerusalem. You are witnesses of these things. And see, I am sending upon you what my Father promised; so stay here in the city until you have been clothed with power from on high.' Then he led them out as far as Bethany, and, lifting up his hands, he blessed them. While he was blessing them, he withdrew from them and was carried up into heaven. And they worshipped him, and returned to Jerusalem with great joy. (Luke 24:46–52)

This is the first of Luke's two accounts of the ascension. While the second (Acts 1) places more emphasis on the developing mission of the church, here we are left with scenes of blessing and 'great joy' (v. 52). Jesus returns to his Father and his followers must wait for the exciting and mysterious 'power from on high' (v. 49).

To me, there is poignancy in the mention of Bethany, where Jesus' dear friends Mary, Martha and Lazarus lived. It was where he had probably been at his most relaxed, a place where he could rest, eat, laugh, cry. What would we not give to have the privilege of knowing the earthly Jesus as closely as that? Yet that relationship had to end, as all such relationships end—through death—and then an infinitely deeper one could develop, which would transform every one of Jesus' followers and, through them, the world.

Both my brothers cried for days when they started school, but eventually found the courage to let go of our mother willingly. They realised that, although they could not see her for a time, she had not vanished for ever. It was the next stage of their growing up. Ascension Day—when, in one sense, the world 'lost' Jesus—points us to Pentecost and the gift of the Holy Spirit to the infant church, bringing courage, love and, most significantly, the energy to continue the process of growing to maturity.

— Reflection —

*'I will not leave you orphaned; I am coming to you'*
*(John 14:18).*

# Making visible the invisible

He is the image of the invisible God, the firstborn of all creation; for in him all things in heaven and on earth were created, things visible and invisible, whether thrones or dominions or rulers or powers—all things have been created through him and for him. He himself is before all things, and in him all things hold together. He is the head of the body, the church; he is the beginning, the firstborn from the dead, so that he might come to have first place in everything. For in him all the fullness of God was pleased to dwell, and through him God was pleased to reconcile to himself all things, whether on earth or in heaven, by making peace through the blood of his cross. (Colossians 1:15–20)

The challenge of these first six readings on God's absence is becoming clear: Jesus died, rose, ascended and sent his Spirit. Therefore, it is now the responsibility of 'the body'—his body, which is the church—to point out to the watching, questioning world that here is the way, the truth and the life (see John 14:6). Over the following readings, we shall reflect on how the church executes that task, and some of the consequences when it fails to do so.

This passage from Colossians reminds us that, in one sense, God is for ever 'absent'. In other words, he is not present in the physical universe in the same way as are we, his creatures. A major part of the sorry history of humanity is our endless striving to generate 'God' in tangible form, something to grasp and shape to our liking. We worship an 'invisible God' but, crucially, we see his exact likeness in his Son, Jesus.

When people demand of us, 'What is your God like?', we can point them to the story of Jesus, as found in scripture. We can also share with them, humbly and hesitantly, whatever experiences we may have had of the love and power of the risen Jesus. Thus, we play our own small part in making the invisible visible.

— Prayer —

*Living Lord, in your mercy use us as your agents*
*of reconciliation.*

# Always forgetting

Thus says the Lord: What wrong did your ancestors find in me that they went far from me, and went after worthless things, and became worthless themselves? They did not say, 'Where is the Lord who brought us up from the land of Egypt, who led us in the wilderness…?' I brought you into a plentiful land to eat its fruits and its good things. But when you entered you defiled my land, and made my heritage an abomination. The priests did not say, 'Where is the Lord?' Those who handle the law did not know me; the rulers transgressed against me; the prophets prophesied by Baal, and went after things that do not profit. (Jeremiah 2:5–8, abridged)

I mentioned before the 'sorry history of humanity'. We now plunge back centuries, to the time of Jeremiah, to remember just how repetitive that history has been. We may lament the state of the church today, but, back then, the 'body' intended as a witness to the Lord Almighty—the nation of Israel—was in desperate straits.

The prophet expresses God's anguish: how could his people forget all that he had done for them? Israel had been chosen for a covenant with the Lord to fulfil the promise to Abraham that, through him, 'all the families of the earth shall be blessed' (Genesis 12:3). Even though God had done his full share of delivering and blessing, his people 'went after worthless things' (Jeremiah 2:5).

This is not so much a case of 'the absence of God' as 'the flight from God'. God is absent because the people have done their utmost to absent themselves from him. Before we condemn, though, we should consider whether we are consciously drawing closer to God's presence or actually trying to escape in some way. For example, do we heed the promptings of conscience—that God-given inner thermostat that warns of spiritual chill—or are we as wilfully disobedient as the long-ago Israelites?

## — Reflection —

*'See, the Lord's hand is not too short to save, nor his ear too dull to hear. Rather, your iniquities have been barriers between you and your God, and your sins have hidden his face from you so that he does not hear' (Isaiah 59:1–2).*

# A personal god

> [The carpenter] plants a cedar and the rain nourishes it. Then it can be used as fuel. Part of it he takes and warms himself; he kindles a fire and bakes bread. Then he makes a god and worships it, makes it a carved image and bows down before it. Half of it he burns in the fire; over this he roasts meat, eats it, and is satisfied. He also warms himself and says, 'Ah, I am warm, I can feel the fire!' The rest of it he makes into a god, his idol, bows down to it, and worships it; he prays to it and says, 'Save me, for you are my god!' (Isaiah 44:14b–17)

I grew up reading missionary stories (my grandparents spent most of their lives in such work) and was fascinated by the idea that many people around the world devoted themselves to 'idol worship'—offering sacrifices (chickens were popular) to scary statues. Over the following years, I heard plenty of sermons pointing out how celebrities, possessions, careers, even friends, can become idols, taking God's place in our hearts.

Being mindful of this, it is still easy to create a false god for ourselves, formed of assumptions, prejudices and half-truths. We shape him to suit our circumstances and worship him, Sunday by Sunday, and, when life does not turn out as we expect, we may turn on this god angrily: 'Why have you let us down? Didn't we say the right words, do the right things?' In our anger, we may think we are facing up to God's absence, but we actually may have to admit that we did not connect with the true God in the first place.

Some would argue for the usefulness of the Anglican

image of a three-legged stool to explain how to understand our faith—the three legs comprising scripture, church tradition and human reason. As we seek to discover more of the true God, this image is a helpful corrective to today's tendency to make things up as we go along, guided by our feelings and, perhaps, the latest Christian teaching from across the Atlantic.

— Prayer —

*God of Abraham, Isaac and Jacob, Father God of all,
grant us a little glimpse of who you truly are.*

# Not doing the job

Thus says the Lord God: Ah, you shepherds of Israel who have been feeding yourselves! Should not shepherds feed the sheep?... You have not strengthened the weak, you have not healed the sick, you have not bound up the injured, you have not brought back the strayed, you have not sought the lost, but with force and harshness you have ruled them... Thus says the Lord God, I am against the shepherds; and I will demand my sheep at their hand... I will rescue my sheep from their mouths, so that they may not be food for them. (Ezekiel 34:2b, 4, 10, abridged)

Here Ezekiel is speaking to those who should have been the godly leaders—the shepherds—of Israel, but were woefully failing in their task. The image of God as shepherd of his people is a familiar one from scripture, but the actual shepherding task was delegated to the ones selected and anointed to be his hands and feet on earth.

It is tempting to read this passage and allow ourselves a little self-satisfied glow as we contemplate the failures of others. The glow might start to fade if we consider exactly how much we have 'strengthened the weak, healed the sick, sought the lost' and so on. As disciples of Jesus, we all have some share in that responsibility, even if we do not lead a church or hold public office. Others tend to judge the Christian faith by the words and deeds of its adherents. What they may see is selfishness, unkindness, arrogance and ongoing battles over various ethical debates that are of secondary importance at best when it comes to proclaiming the gospel message.

Those of us who have the daunting privilege of leadership should remember that kindness, rather than perfectly correct doctrine, is what may well speak loudest to those outside the church. The rest of us should pray for our leaders and, where appropriate, remind them of the importance of caring for their flock rather than simply grandstanding on 'issues'.

## — Reflection —

*Jesus said, 'I am the good shepherd. The good shepherd lays down his life for his sheep' (John 10:11). What might this mean in practice for those called to lead God's people today?*

# God at a distance

Why, O Lord, do you stand far off? Why do you hide yourself in times of trouble? In arrogance the wicked persecute the poor—let them be caught in the schemes they have devised. For the wicked boast of the desires of their heart, those greedy for gain curse and renounce the Lord. In the pride of their countenance the wicked say, 'God will not seek it out'; all their thoughts are, 'There is no God.'… They think in their heart, 'God has forgotten, he has hidden his face, he will never see it.' (Psalm 10:1–4, 11)

Sebastian Faulks' novel *A Week in December* includes one of the most chilling characters in recent fiction. John Veals is a man to whom adjectives such as 'manipulative', 'calculating' and 'ruthless' barely begin to do justice. He is an enormously successful, utterly unscrupulous city financier who, with a few phone calls, can close deals resulting in ruin for whole countries. He becomes even wealthier; the poor are crushed.

The psalmist despairs at God's absence in the face of deliberate wickedness (as opposed to natural disasters, such as earthquakes and tsunamis, which are not a direct consequence of human behaviour). It is less a case of 'Is there a God?' than 'Why is he keeping such a low profile?' After all, if (as many believe) God still intervenes today to heal, give prophetic words and touch individual lives, why can he not take direct action to stop evil people doing their worst?

The inescapable answer is 'free will'. Human beings have the God-given capability to choose, and, although we often make good choices, there are too many times when our choices lead to harm. If we seek to live as God's children, our calling is to do all we can to remind the world—and the church—of the values of God's kingdom as found throughout scripture: caring for the poor, working for equitable economic systems, protecting the environment, revealing God's love to others. God is not hiding; he is waiting for us to take action.

## — Reflection —

*These may be familiar words, but they remain powerfully true: 'The only thing necessary for the triumph of evil is for good men to do nothing.'*
Attributed to Edmund Burke (1729–97)

# The last hope

When Mary came where Jesus was and saw him, she knelt at his feet and said to him, 'Lord, if you had been here, my brother would not have died.' When Jesus saw her weeping, and the Jews who came with her also weeping, he was greatly disturbed in spirit and deeply moved. He said, 'Where have you laid him?' They said to him, 'Lord, come and see.' Jesus began to weep. So the Jews said, 'See how he loved him!' But some of them said, 'Could not he who opened the eyes of the blind man have kept this man from dying?' (John 11:32–37)

In contrast to the last two readings, in this passage we see the point beyond which no human action is of any use. Mary's brother is dead. The Son of God failed to turn up and, when he finally does come, it is seemingly too late for anything except bitter tears. Even today, in an era of extraordinary medical advances, the moment always comes when death is inevitable, when earthly help is exhausted. We turn to prayer, which may have been our first hope but is also surely always our last... and the answer seems to be either negative or just silence.

The pain is unspeakable—and close on the heels of pain comes anger. Even as Jesus shakes with grief at the loss of Lazarus, some of those watching respond with anger. He could have made a difference; he did not; he obviously did not care so very much.

Jesus' passionate response to the horror of death is to bring his friend back to life, showing that the kingdom of heaven is unstoppable and offering a foretaste of the future resurrection promised to all. In the light of this miracle and (even more so) his own resurrection life, we need not fear being cut off from God by the grave. Knowing this, though, we must still wait for the full consequences to unfold. As we live in this in-between time, we have to trust that the Father's love is strong and real enough to hold us in our tear-streaked misery.

## — Reflection —

*'You have kept count of my tossings; put my tears in your bottle' (Psalm 56:8).*

# Waiting for the Lord

Out of the depths I cry to you, O Lord. Lord, hear my voice!
Let your ears be attentive to the voice of my supplications! If
you, O Lord, should mark iniquities, Lord, who could stand?
But there is forgiveness with you, so that you may be revered.
I wait for the Lord, my soul waits, and in his word I hope;
my soul waits for the Lord more than those who watch for
the morning, more than those who watch for the morning.
O Israel, hope in the Lord! For with the Lord there is steadfast
love, and with him is great power to redeem. It is he who will
redeem Israel from all its iniquities. (Psalm 130)

Here we find despair at God's absence, mingled with hope.
The psalmist calls from 'the depths' (v. 1). By contrast with
Psalm 139, he does not seem able to sense the presence of the
Lord with him in that place of terror and turmoil.

A child secure in the knowledge that they are loved has a
pretty much unshakeable confidence that if they cry out in
fear in the night, somebody will come and comfort them. This
does not make their fear any less real and their crying may
still be desperate, but the certainty of consolation sustains
them, even as they listen out for the footsteps on the stairs.

We might hazard a guess from the psalmist's mention of
'iniquities' and 'forgiveness' that he ended up in the depths as
a result of his own actions. He feels far from God's presence,
floundering in darkness, but still has enough strength to hold
on to what he knows to be true: the Lord is both loving and
redeeming, not only to individuals but also to whole nations,
even when they have done wrong. Despite the gulf between

himself and God, he refuses to give up hope. As surely as the
sun rises, he knows that, in the end, he will be saved.

## — Reflection —

*'I believe that I shall see the goodness of the Lord in the land
of the living. Wait for the Lord; be strong, and let your heart
take courage; wait for the Lord!' (Psalm 27:13–14).*

# Hidden glory

I consider that the sufferings of this present time are not worth comparing with the glory about to be revealed to us... We know that the whole creation has been groaning in labour pains until now; and not only the creation, but we ourselves, who have the first fruits of the Spirit, groan inwardly while we wait for adoption, the redemption of our bodies. For in hope we were saved. Now hope that is seen is not hope. For who hopes for what is seen? But if we hope for what we do not see, we wait for it with patience. (Romans 8:18, 22–25)

Reading this passage, we should remember that, in referring to labour pains, Paul is not thinking of the sort of groans associated with waking and stretching in the morning. Nor is he talking about waiting as a kind of 'Ho hum, this is taking a while' feeling. He meant to evoke a kind of intense pain that overwhelms all thought, all perspective and any awareness that it will come to an end.

We are waiting for the completion of God's work of salvation, the full realisation of the resurrection hope of Easter and the final outworking of the promise of Pentecost. As we saw in a previous reading, this in-between time can be dominated by pain, suffering and loss, but it is also suffused with hope. In God's good time, we hope that everything will be brought to completion; we will see him face to face; his glory will be visible to every eye. As Jesus pointed out, when a baby is born, the pain of giving birth is forgotten (John 16:21). When our redemption is complete, the ache and longing that may fill our hearts now will shrink to nothing.

Meanwhile, as we groan and wait and try to be patient, we can join with God's work in the world, doing faithfully and obediently whatever is given us to do. We may fear we will never see the end result, the pay-off for our efforts, but that is why both hope and patience are so vital for our ongoing journey through life.

## — Prayer —

*Lord God, grant us not only your transcendent peace but also a measure of your infinite patience.*

# Into the darkness

And when the priests came out of the holy place, a cloud filled the house of the Lord, so that the priests could not stand to minister because of the cloud; for the glory of the Lord filled the house of the Lord. Then Solomon said, 'The Lord has said that he would dwell in thick darkness. I have built you an exalted house, a place for you to dwell in for ever.' (1 Kings 8:10–13)

Our final reading in this series comes from the dedication of Solomon's temple. After the ark of the covenant had been installed in the most 'holy place' (v. 10) and the priests had withdrawn, the cloud of God's glory filled the place. A footnote in the NRSV links Solomon's words to Psalm 97, where God is described as surrounded by swirling cloud, darkness and lightning, just as at Sinai when the Law was first given to Moses.

All such descriptions are, in the end, fumbling attempts to use human language and earthly imagery to express the inexpressible and describe the indescribable. Over the centuries, many Christians have come to a point where they feel it is easier to try and grasp something of God by defining what he is not, rather than what he is. Known as the *via negativa*, or 'negative way', this has been given a stronger emphasis in Eastern Christian traditions, especially the Orthodox Church.

Yes, of course, we believe that we find God in scripture and the church and supremely revealed in Jesus Christ, but we can never hope to encompass the eternal with our finite minds. Instead, we can dare to step out into the darkness, beyond the borders of knowledge and understanding and what we think we know about God. We can dare to venture deeper and deeper into his presence, willing to hold open our hands to whatever he will give us, admitting our emptiness so that his Spirit can truly fill us, remembering that his apparent absence is simply the shadow cast by his immense and unavoidable presence.

## — Reflection —

*'I will give you the treasures of darkness and riches hidden in secret places, so that you may know that it is I, the Lord, the God of Israel, who call you by your name' (Isaiah 45:3).*

# — Part 2 —
# Challenged to journey

When we sense God's call to move on, his summons to take up the work that he has prepared for us to do, we may fear that we are moving from a place of coping (even if it is coping at the level of drawing one breath after another) to what will prove to be a (literally) breathtaking series of challenges. Survival is one thing, which we may have learned to do quite well, but stepping out in the service of the kingdom of heaven may prove a different level of daunting. The questions hammer away at us. How will we know the right way to take? Can we trust that what we perceive as God's guidance is actually just that? What if we accidentally take a wrong turning and find ourselves in a spiritual dead end?

The readings in this next section are, in part, reflections on the costliness of obedience to God's call. Jonah the reluctant prophet, Stephen the first martyr and Jesus himself walked in that obedience (eventually, it must be said, in the case of Jonah), even when it proved immensely costly. For Stephen and Jesus, it cost everything, including life itself.

We may fear that God will ask us to do more than we can possibly manage, but we have to trust that where he calls, there he will also provide the necessary gifts, wisdom and energy. Our task is to quieten our hearts so that we can hear his voice and, as in the following poem, seek to know beyond doubt that this is indeed the way we should go.

# Kairos

What if he came now,
Riding the stormclouds
From the west
As high winds
Whip up the white-tops
And curtains of rain are
Torn in two—
Top to bottom—
While sunlight dazzles everywhere
In haloes of spray?

But will I recognise him?
Will I blink and miss the moment
So it all moves on
Without me,
The strategic hour passing,
The right move
Unmade?

All I can do is this:
Watch the skyline,
Walk the sea-margin,
Shoes scuffing the sand,
And wait
In faith
In hope
That when he calls,
I'll know his voice
For sure.

# Introduction
## Bible stories rediscovered: Jonah

Along with Noah and the ark, Jonah and the whale is one of the best-known Old Testament stories. It is such a small but perfectly formed narrative, with fast-paced action, snappy dialogue, dramatic shifts in scene and, above all, that monstrous sea creature rearing up from the deep to save the (anti-)hero at the eleventh hour.

I hope that, before starting this series of readings, you will take a few moments to read the whole book at a sitting (it is just 48 verses, four short chapters), if only to realise that the 'big fish' is not identified as a whale at all and, in fact, takes up only three verses.

Jonah, the most reluctant of prophets, also appears in 2 Kings 14:25, where he is identified as coming 'from Gath-hepher'. Jesus mentions 'the sign of Jonah' in Matthew 12:39–41 and 16:4, as well as Luke 11:29–32. In the first of the passages in Matthew, he draws a comparison between Jonah's sojourn in the 'belly of the sea monster' and the three days and nights that 'the Son of Man' will spend 'in the heart of the earth'.

'Did it really happen, though?' some may ask. That may not be a particularly helpful question in relation to this story. Some might stubbornly argue that God can do anything he likes, including providing piscatorial rescue services. What is at the heart of the adventures of Jonah, however, is not a question of historicity (or lack of it), but what we learn about God and humanity.

Commentators tend to describe Jonah in disparaging terms

and he is seldom held up as a good example of prophetic witness, but, in fact, Jonah is no worse—and, in many ways, a good deal braver—than the rest of us. We should not feel superior to him, but acknowledge how, like us, he fails and fails and fails again, yet God uses him to achieve a work so amazing that Jonah struggles to comprehend it.

The readings that follow, then, are for those of us who are keenly aware of our personal failings. Like Jonah, we can be humbled to find that, in God's mercy and grace, we can still play some small part in building his kingdom.

# Runaway prophet

Now the word of the Lord came to Jonah son of Amittai, saying, 'Go at once to Nineveh, that great city, and cry out against it; for their wickedness has come up before me.' But Jonah set out to flee to Tarshish from the presence of the Lord. He went down to Joppa and found a ship going to Tarshish; so he paid his fare and went on board, to go with them to Tarshish, away from the presence of the Lord. (Jonah 1:1–3)

Jonah's 'reluctant prophet' credentials are established here as, instead of heeding the word of the Lord, he embarks on a futile escape attempt. The location of Tarshish is unclear, but, as the name derives from the word for 'sea', it could refer to somewhere on the Mediterranean. Jonah is heading in precisely the opposite direction to inland Nineveh. His desperation is perhaps reflected in his trying to flee by ship—a highly dubious enterprise from the perspective of a non-seagoing nation such as Israel.

He had some reason for his desperation. Nineveh was the capital of the Assyrian empire, and the Assyrians are generally considered to have been among the most brutal conquerors in the ancient world. They were notorious for wiping out their opponents, but not before they had tormented and humiliated them in some spectacularly unpleasant ways. At least the later Babylonians and Persians allowed defeated nations a modicum of self-rule. Also, the Lord told Jonah not to denounce this evil empire from a safe distance but actually to go there to declaim against its wickedness.

This passage also points towards one of the main themes

in Jonah—the inescapable presence of the Lord. We can hold before God the memory of those who died in conflict and thank him that his power, love and mercy are greater even than the grave.

## — Reflection —

*'If I ascend to heaven, you are there; if I make my bed in Sheol, you are there. If I take the wings of the morning and settle at the farthest limits of the sea, even there your hand shall lead me, and your right hand shall hold me fast'*
*(Psalm 139:8–10).*

# No escape

But the Lord hurled a great wind upon the sea, and such a
mighty storm came upon the sea that the ship threatened to
break up. Then the mariners were afraid, and each cried to
his god... Jonah, meanwhile, had gone down into the hold of
the ship and had lain down, and was fast asleep... The sailors
said to one another, 'Come, let us cast lots, so that we may
know on whose account this calamity has come upon us.' So
they cast lots, and the lot fell on Jonah. Then they said to him
'... What is this that you have done!' For the men knew that
he was fleeing from the presence of the Lord, because he had
told them so. (Jonah 1:4–5, 7–8, 10, abridged)

Have you ever been in a small boat on a stormy sea? Even if
the wind has died down, the swell can stay heavy for hours
and we may fear a sudden rogue wave swamping us. The
sailors here face such a 'great wind' and 'mighty storm' that
all hope seems lost. If you have not already done so, read
this passage in full so as to appreciate the narrator's skill in
evoking the scene, the desperate emotional state of the crew
mirroring the tempest raging around them.

The sleep of Jonah has been characterised on the one hand
as smug somnolence and, on the other, as exhaustion, the
depressed mental state of a man who has cut his ties to his
old life, including trying to run away from his God. Perhaps
what he feels is simply relief; he hopes that he has escaped
after all. Despite the fearful sea crossing to be endured, new
opportunities may be opening ahead.

Then his secret is discovered. With horrible inevitability,

the 'lot' picks him out as the cause of the tempest. Jonah is about to learn just how inescapable God is—and also how compassionate—but his journey will take him literally through very deep waters first. Sometimes for us, too, life gets a whole lot worse before we sense any hint of the skies starting to clear.

## — Reflection —

*O hear us when we cry to Thee for those in peril on the sea!*
William Whiting (1860)

# Saving many or saving one?

> Then [the sailors] said to him, 'What shall we do to you, that
> the sea may quieten down for us?'... He said to them, 'Pick
> me up and throw me into the sea; then the sea will quieten
> down for you; for I know it is because of me that this great
> storm has come upon you.'... So they picked Jonah up and
> threw him into the sea; and the sea ceased from its raging.
> Then the men feared the Lord even more, and they offered a
> sacrifice to the Lord and made vows. But the Lord provided
> a large fish to swallow up Jonah; and Jonah was in the belly
> of the fish for three days and three nights. (Jonah 1:11–12,
> 15–17, abridged)

I struggled with shortening this passage because it is easy
to give an unfair impression of the sailors. From the words
given above, it sounds as if they were quick to rid themselves
of their troublesome passenger. In fact, though, verses 13–14
tell how they first struggled to bring the ship to land and,
when that failed, prayed to Jonah's God not to punish them
for the human sacrifice that now appeared inevitable.

Jonah's willingness to be sacrificed (v. 12) is an indication,
surely, that he is not quite the complete no-hoper that is
sometimes portrayed. The consequent miraculous calming
of the storm serves to strengthen the sailors' fledgling faith
and is a foretaste of the mass repentance that God will bring
about through Jonah's preaching when he finally reaches
Nineveh.

There is a poignant scene in the film *Master and Commander:
the Far Side of the World* (2003) where a broken mast catapults

a sailor into the waves. To save the ship from capsizing, the captain is forced to leave the man behind. We then see the ship from the perspective of the drowning man, racing away further and further over the mountainous sea. That was Jonah's plight, but then along comes the most unlikely of rescuers. Unlike any other god, the Lord can control not only the weather and the waves but also the sea creatures. Now he acts to save his prophet.

— Reflection —

*Never to fall into despair, but into God.*
Olivier Clément (1921–2009)

# Snatched from the grave

Then Jonah prayed to the Lord his God from the belly of
the fish, saying, 'I called to the Lord out of my distress, and
he answered me; out of the belly of Sheol I cried, and you
heard my voice... The waters closed in over me; the deep
surrounded me; weeds were wrapped around my head at
the roots of the mountains. I went down to the land whose
bars closed upon me for ever; yet you brought up my life
from the Pit, O Lord my God. As my life was ebbing away,
I remembered the Lord; and my prayer came to you, into
your holy temple... Deliverance belongs to the Lord!' Then
the Lord spoke to the fish, and it spewed Jonah out upon the
dry land. (Jonah 2:1–2, 5–7, 9–10, abridged)

There is a vivid description of drowning in *The Perfect Storm*
by Sebastian Junger (1999), a book (later filmed) about a
particularly terrifying 1991 hurricane. Even as the body's
systems are shutting down from lack of oxygen, the will
to live continues to assert itself and an inner voice pleads,
'How can it end like this?' Such a description can only be
written because people are sometimes pulled back from that
particular grave, surviving to tell how it was.

Jonah had thought that his end had truly come and his
words give a chilling sense of being lost far beneath the waves,
tangled up in seaweed. The prayer has a similar emotional
progression to that found in psalms of thanksgiving: a
description of how God answered the speaker's prayers,
a summary of the crisis and the divine deliverance, con-
cluding with a promise of future acts of thanksgiving.

Whether the crisis has threatened physical death or other personal catastrophe, the feelings of the delivered one are an exhilarating mixture of relief, astonishment, joy and disbelief, with, perhaps, a hint of survivor's guilt.

Many who survive disaster speak of a sense of being given another chance, a second go at life. Jonah has acknowledged that he is helpless in God's merciful hands; now he will have the chance to serve the Lord again.

— Reflection —

*'I believe that I shall see the goodness of the Lord in the land of the living' (Psalm 27:13).*

# Mission unbelievable

The word of the Lord came to Jonah a second time, saying,
'Get up, go to Nineveh, that great city, and proclaim to it the
message that I tell you.'... Now Nineveh was an exceedingly
large city, a three days' walk across. Jonah began to go into
the city, going a day's walk. And he cried out, 'Forty days
more, and Nineveh shall be overthrown!' And the people of
Nineveh believed God; they proclaimed a fast, and everyone,
great and small, put on sackcloth. When the news reached
the king of Nineveh, he rose from his throne, removed his
robe, covered himself with sackcloth and sat in ashes. (Jonah
3:1–6, abridged)

The prophet's journey begins again, this time in the direction
of obedience, taking him into the heart of a bloated metropolis.
Even to reach Nineveh would have been an arduous trek
from Israel, giving Jonah plenty of time for second, third and
fourth thoughts, but he does not turn back and, when he
finally arrives, he obediently begins his prophetic task. So,
does a mob surround this impertinent foreigner and stone
him to death? Or is it the case that no one pays the slightest
attention, even though he preaches until his voice is hoarse
and his heart broken?

Er, no. What actually happens next is enough to make
any stadium evangelist green with envy—a repentance rate
more dramatic than the crowd's response to Peter's sermon
at Pentecost (when there were a measly 3000 converts: Acts
2:41). Everybody, but everybody in Nineveh, from the king
to the cattle, puts on sackcloth and embarks on a total fast,

desperately hoping that it is not too late to avert disaster.

For God to use us for his redeeming work in the world, we do not need to be fearless campaigners, superb intellects or polished public speakers. We certainly do not need to be morally flawless either, but we do need to be willing to submit to God's loving guidance. If we are prepared to take such a momentous step of obedience as Jonah took, who knows what might happen?

— Reflection —

*'Then I heard the voice of the Lord saying, "Whom shall I send, and who will go for us?" And I said, "Here I am; send me!"' (Isaiah 6:8).*

# Mercy immeasurable

When God saw what they did, how they turned from their evil ways, God changed his mind about the calamity that he had said he would bring upon them; and he did not do it. But this was very displeasing to Jonah, and he became angry. He prayed to the Lord and said, 'O Lord! Is not this what I said while I was still in my own country? That is why I fled to Tarshish at the beginning; for I knew that you are a gracious God…' Then Jonah went out of the city… and made a booth for himself there. He sat under it in the shade, waiting to see what would become of the city. (Jonah 3:10—4:2, 5, abridged)

This passage is just one of so many that shine through the scriptures—when transgression is pardoned, humiliation meets mercy, and brokenness is made whole. God cares passionately about wrongdoing but he is equally passionate about forgiveness. This is what upsets Jonah, because it seems as if his entire trip was pointless. 'God was going to forgive Nineveh anyway, so why drag me into it?' he is thinking.

What matters is that the people had the chance to repent. Of course God was ready to forgive, but, for the forgiveness to take effect, releasing healing and restoration, the wrongdoers had to acknowledge that something needed to be mended. They had to open themselves to heavenly mercy, and that was where Jonah came in. The prophet's job was to confront them with the mess they were in, because, although God's grace and mercy are eternal, they are never forced on unwilling recipients.

Forgiveness is always an amazing, miraculous work of God. We may know we deeply regret something that we have done to another, but it may feel too risky to confess and apologise. A thoughtful, careful and sensitive apology—face to face if possible—shows not only that we are truly sorry but also that we acknowledge the consequences of our actions for the other person. We may feel that apologising shatters our careful emotional barriers, but, if the other person tells us that we are forgiven, it can be a profound moment of healing.

— Reflection —

*'While we still were sinners Christ died for us' (Romans 5:8).*

# Love unimaginable

The Lord God appointed a bush, and made it come up over Jonah, to give shade over his head... so Jonah was very happy about the bush. But when dawn came up the next day, God appointed a worm that attacked the bush, so that it withered. When the sun rose, God prepared a sultry east wind, and the sun beat down on the head of Jonah so that he was faint and asked that he might die... God said to Jonah, 'Is it right for you to be angry about the bush?' And he said, 'Yes, angry enough to die.' Then the Lord said, 'You are concerned about the bush... should I not be concerned about Nineveh, that great city...?' (Jonah 4:6–11, abridged)

Jonah cannot grasp the ways of God; the prophetic task has brought him nothing but anguish. What finishes him is the withering of the plant that offered some respite from the searing desert heat. Parched beyond endurance, he decides that he has had enough. Then God comes to him, not in a blaze of fury but in a patient righting of perspective. Jonah must look up from his grief over a dead plant and realise that his feelings are only the slightest shadow of the grief and compassion God feels for his children.

Life may seem desperate; no matter where we look, we may see no prospect of escape from our circumstances. Whether or not this is really true, we need not give way to hopelessness. Instead, we can hold fast to the truth—the rope hauling us from the pit—that there can be no end to the infinite Father. He loves and cares and forgives more than we can ever imagine.

What of Nineveh? That huge city had been so comprehensively destroyed by 612BC that the Greek historian Xenophon walked past without noticing it. Forgiveness can be the beginning—or continuation—of our walk with God or something that we start to forget and take for granted. That was the choice faced by the people of Nineveh and that is our choice today.

— Reflection —

*'I have set before you life and death, blessings and curses.*
*Choose life so that you and your descendants may live'*
*(Deuteronomy 30:19).*

# Introduction
## Stephen's speech (Acts 7:2−53)

It is good to be able to spend time focusing on the speech made by Stephen, the first Christian martyr. As the church calendar sets his feast day on 26 December, his full story is too easily missed in the post-Christmas haze.

We may think of his death simply as the precursor to Saul's dramatic conversion on the road to Damascus (9:1–19), but, in fact, if we look at his lengthy speech before his accusers, we see a fascinating contrast with Peter's earlier sermon at Pentecost (2:14–35). Whereas Peter explains the gospel message with a series of Old Testament (Hebrew Bible) texts, Stephen retells the story of God's dealings with Israel, from the first call to Abraham to the building of Solomon's temple.

Similar retellings crop up in numerous places in scripture—the book of Deuteronomy, Psalms 105 and 106 (among others), Hebrews 11—considering what God has done in the past to provide encouragement or shape rightful attitudes for the future. Stephen has been accused of 'saying things against this holy place [the temple] and the law' (Acts 6:13) and so, in his defence, he tells this story to show how God has been at work over the centuries, above all through the leadership of Moses. At the same time, God's people have consistently rebelled against him. Most shockingly, Stephen goes on to question the very basis of the temple's founding: was it a divine requirement or an essentially human initiative?

The Greek word *martus*, from which we get the English 'martyr', means 'witness'. This has come to have the primary meaning of one so committed to a cause or truth that they are prepared to die rather than deny it. They willingly renounce the chance of seeing whether or not their cause or truth triumphs but are sustained in their suffering by the hope that their sacrifice will bear fruit, somehow, some day. We have to read beyond Stephen's speech, to Acts 8:1, before we see a hint that his death was not fruitless.

In writing on these passages, I have been helped by two commentaries on Acts: Loveday Alexander's *People's Bible Commentary: Acts* (BRF, 2006) and David J. Williams' *Acts: New International Biblical Commentary* (Hendrickson, 1995).

# Called to hope

Stephen replied: 'Brothers and fathers, listen to me. The God of glory appeared to our ancestor Abraham when he was in Mesopotamia, before he lived in Haran, and said to him, "Leave your country and your relatives and go to the land that I will show you." Then he left the country of the Chaldeans and settled in Haran. After his father died, God had him move from there to this country in which you are now living. He did not give him any of it as a heritage, not even a foot's length, but promised to give it to him as his possession and to his descendants after him, even though he had no child.' (Acts 7:2–5)

In the opening words of Stephen's speech, he reminds his audience that the story he tells links directly to the present moment. He appeals to his 'brothers and fathers', as, though they may have been sitting in judgement on him, they are all children of the originally childless Abraham and the place where they are sitting is in the land promised to their forefather. He is saying that the fact they are gathered there at all speaks of the sovereignty and faithfulness of God.

Throughout his speech, Stephen condenses the original stories to highlight his message. As Loveday Alexander puts it, 'Stephen's potted history emphasises the coming out more than the eventual destination, the letting go of certainties more than the acquisition of new possessions' (pp. 58–59). Abraham is the starting point, not because his entire life was exemplary (far from it), but because the promises made to him mark the origin of Israel's existence as a people with a special relationship with God.

Abraham is commended in Hebrews 11:10 for his faith: 'He looked forward to the city that has foundations, whose architect and builder is God.' His example reminds us that if we submit our lives in obedience to God, we must be content to play our part—however hidden it may be—in his universal purposes rather than clamour impatiently to see the end of the story.

— Prayer —

*Grant us a breadth of vision, O God, so that we remember you are Lord of all time and space, not just of our own little concerns.*

# Called to belong

'And God spoke in these terms, that his descendants would be resident aliens in a country belonging to others, who would enslave them and mistreat them for four hundred years. "But I will judge the nation that they serve," said God, "and after that they shall come out and worship me in this place." Then he gave him the covenant of circumcision. And so Abraham became the father of Isaac and circumcised him on the eighth day; and Isaac became the father of Jacob, and Jacob of the twelve patriarchs.' (Acts 7:6–8)

It comes as a shock to hear that God's promise to Abraham includes the 400 years of suffering and slavery endured by the Israelites in Egypt. The point is, however, not that God wilfully inflicts pain to serve a greater good but that he is omnipotent, despite any indication to the contrary. The warning of suffering is tempered by a promise of judgement on the tyrant nation of Egypt, although so many would have died long before that judgement would come to pass.

Interestingly, the exodus is presented not as an 'escape to the true homeland' but 'being set free to worship'. This sentiment echoes Zechariah's song (itself a mini-retelling of the God–Israel story) at the circumcision of John the Baptist, where he speaks of how 'we, being rescued from the hands of our enemies, might serve [the Lord God] without fear, in holiness and righteousness before him all our days' (Luke 1:74–75). The fundamental point of the covenant is not so much possession of the land as the relationship with God that the land symbolises.

God's disclosure to Abraham concludes here with 'the covenant of circumcision'. This was the sign of belonging for the people of God (for the men, anyway) and Stephen's words are a reminder that this sign predated both the law given to Moses and the building of the temple—the two things he has been accused of denigrating. He is perhaps hinting at what his accusers fail to perceive: God is greater than they know and his agenda encompasses more than they can possibly understand.

— Reflection —

*What do you think should be the sign of belonging to the people of God today?*

# Called far from home

'The patriarchs, jealous of Joseph, sold him into Egypt; but God was with him, and rescued him from all his afflictions, and enabled him to win favour and to show wisdom when he stood before Pharaoh, king of Egypt, who appointed him ruler over Egypt and over all his household. Now there came a famine throughout Egypt and Canaan, and great suffering, and our ancestors could find no food. But when Jacob heard that there was grain in Egypt, he sent our ancestors there on their first visit. On the second visit Joseph made himself known to his brothers, and Joseph's family became known to Pharaoh.' (Acts 7:9–13)

Like Daniel and Esther after him, Joseph ends up prospering in exile. Thanks to the sovereign workings of God, he is the right person in the right place at the right time, blessed with wisdom not only to help his own people but also to benefit the community that, for him, is one far from home. A key realisation to come out of the years of Jewish exile in Babylon was that God is not a local deity, limited to a specific territory or sacred location: his authority extends to the ends of the earth.

Joseph's experiences are also a reminder that the patriarchal family was often characterised by rivalry, bitter in-fighting and even violence: 'Stephen reminds his audience that the history of God's people is a history of jealousy and rejection within the family' (Alexander, p. 59). Such, too, was the experience of Jesus, who commented ruefully, 'Prophets are not without honour, except in their home town, and among their own kin, and in their own house' (Mark 6:4). We should remember that Stephen is speaking a relatively short time after Jesus was rejected by his own people—a rejection that led to his violent death. The audience would have been more than a little sensitive to any suggestion that a pattern might be discernible here.

## — Reflection —

*'No weapon that is fashioned against you shall prosper, and you shall confute every tongue that rises against you in judgement. This is the heritage of the servants of the Lord and their vindication from me, says the Lord' (Isaiah 54:17).*

# Grave errors?

'Then Joseph sent and invited his father Jacob and all his relatives to come to him, seventy-five in all; so Jacob went down to Egypt. He himself died there as well as our ancestors, and their bodies were brought back to Shechem and laid in the tomb that Abraham had bought for a sum of silver from the sons of Hamor in Shechem.' (Acts 7:14–16)

At this point, we may pause in puzzlement. If Stephen is summarising the sweep of Jewish history in the closing moments of his life, why so much detail about who was buried where? Also, commentators point out that his narrative seems to confuse two burial stories. Genesis 50:13 says that Jacob was buried on the land bought by Abraham at Hebron (see 23:15–19); Joshua 24:32 tells us that Joseph's bones were brought from Egypt for burial at Shechem, on land bought by Jacob (Genesis 33:19). The Old Testament does not mention where his brothers were buried.

The thought that the Bible contains factual inaccuracies may be very troubling for some, but it is undeniable. Of course it is the inspired word of God, but it was written down by humans (and, here, spoken by a human) and humans sometimes make mistakes or present information in a less than straightforward way! This does not detract in any way from the overall authority of scripture, and admitting that there is the occasional error need not diminish our reverence for the text and the truths that it contains.

As to why Stephen should include details about these graves, we can surely understand it if we think of the astonishing rise in the popularity of family history research that has occurred in recent years. Churches constantly field calls from those asking about long-ago baptisms, weddings and funerals and whether or not graves can be visited. People want to know about their roots, to affirm 'This is where I come from', even 'This is where part of me belongs.' In death, so Stephen tells us, the patriarchs were brought back to rest in the land given them by God. So, these details matter because belonging matters.

## — Prayer —

*O Lord God, thank you for your holy scriptures.*
*Help us to read them with clear eyes, reverence and*
*willingness to receive your word to us each day.*

# Beautiful before God

'But as the time drew near for the fulfilment of the promise that God had made to Abraham, our people in Egypt increased and multiplied until another king who had not known Joseph ruled over Egypt. He dealt craftily with our race and forced our ancestors to abandon their infants so that they would die. At this time Moses was born, and he was beautiful before God. For three months he was brought up in his father's house; and when he was abandoned, Pharaoh's daughter adopted him and brought him up as her own son. So Moses was instructed in all the wisdom of the Egyptians and was powerful in his words and deeds.' (Acts 7:17–22)

The lovely phrase used as our title is the way the infant Moses is portrayed in Stephen's speech. Exodus 2:2 talks of him as a 'fine baby' (I also like the KJV's 'goodly child'), but the particularly poetic choice of words here is characteristic of the generally heightened picture of Moses that Stephen presents. It is interesting to read of him as 'powerful in his words and deeds' because, in Exodus 4:10, Moses says that he is 'slow of speech and slow of tongue'—but perhaps we should allow him some modesty in his description of himself!

Why does Stephen present Moses in this way? We should remember the context of this speech. Stephen has been accused of rejecting the law that God gave to Israel through Moses and so, by extension, rejecting Moses himself. In his retelling of Moses' life, he shows that, on the contrary, he fully endorses his place as the greatest figure in Israel's history.

The bigger story is coming to its first climax, with the promise to Abraham and the move to Egypt leading to a crisis when genocide looks to be the unavoidable fate of God's people. At such a time of danger, God chooses a mere baby who will grow up—blessed with heavenly wisdom, strength and courage—to be a saviour. There are clear parallels with the life of Jesus, but they are tactfully implicit so as not to undermine Moses. They are mere echoes but ones that the perceptive hearer will notice and understand.

— Prayer —

*Thank you, Lord God, that we are all beautiful in your eyes.*

# Mishearing the call

'When [Moses] was forty years old, it came into his heart to visit his relatives, the Israelites. When he saw one of them being wronged, he... avenged him by striking down the Egyptian. He supposed that his kinsfolk would understand that God through him was rescuing them, but they did not understand. The next day he came to some of them as they were quarrelling and tried to reconcile them, saying, "Men, you are brothers; why do you wrong each other?" But the man who was wronging his neighbour pushed Moses aside, saying, "Who made you a ruler and a judge over us? Do you want to kill me as you killed the Egyptian yesterday?" When he heard this, Moses fled and became a resident alien in the land of Midian. There he became the father of two sons.' (Acts 7:23–29, abridged)

We are told that Moses' desire to reconnect with his relatives 'came into his heart', suggesting that it was a work of God rather than his own instinct. The call to serve and save comes as he reaches the age of 40 (although the Old Testament offers no evidence for this figure). What happens, though, is that he misunderstands how the call should work out in practice. Living in an oppressive society, where slavery and violence are part of everyday life, means that Moses' automatic response to conflict is one of violence.

The story shows the central importance for any would-be servant of God of cultivating attitudes of patience, humility and obedience. If we simply stride out—or hit out—in our strength, powered by our own assumptions about the 'right thing to do', we will probably end up in a mess, later if not sooner. Praying faithfully and expectantly for a situation or person involves bringing our concerns and requests into God's loving presence and waiting, in silence, for his response, which may take much longer and come in a very different way than we expect.

## — Reflection —

*All of a sudden we just know: prayer is a conversation in which God's word has the initiative and we, for the moment, can be nothing more than listeners.*

Hans Urs von Balthasar, *Prayer* (Ignatius Press, 1986)

# A voice in the desert

'Now when forty years had passed, an angel appeared to [Moses] in the wilderness of Mount Sinai, in the flame of a burning bush. When Moses saw it, he was amazed at the sight; and as he approached to look, there came the voice of the Lord: "I am the God of your ancestors, the God of Abraham, Isaac and Jacob." Moses began to tremble and did not dare to look. Then the Lord said to him, "Take off the sandals from your feet, for the place where you are standing is holy ground. I have surely seen the mistreatment of my people who are in Egypt and have heard their groaning, and I have come down to rescue them. Come now, I will send you to Egypt."' (Acts 7:30–34)

Moses had to turn his back on his comfortable upbringing among the Egyptian ruling class in order to discern God's call correctly. He ends up spending years with the desert-dwelling Midianites, even marrying and raising a family there. Such 'wilderness time' can seem very daunting, when we find ourselves far from familiar routines and landmarks, and we may worry that we have lost our bearings altogether. Perhaps that is what needs to happen, though, for us to begin to work out who we really are and what we ought to do with our lives. It is only then that we can begin to tune into the gentle whisper of God.

Just as Joseph knew the Lord's presence with him in prison in Egypt, so now Moses hears God at an apparently random site in the barren hills—one that is about as different as imaginable from the grand monuments of the Nile valley.

That inauspicious place becomes holy ground, as he realises that he is actually in the presence of God. Finally, Moses understands who is calling him, where he is being called to and what his task will be—a moment as pivotal as the original call to Abraham.

## — Reflection —

*'We are fallen in mostly broken pieces… but the wild can still return us to ourselves' (Robert Macfarlane,* The Wild Places, *Granta, 2007). Where in your life are the 'wild places' where you can pause to be open to God?*

# Despised and rejected

'It was this Moses whom [the people] rejected when they said, "Who made you a ruler and a judge?" and whom God now sent as both ruler and liberator through the angel who appeared to him in the bush. He led them out, having performed wonders and signs in Egypt, at the Red Sea, and in the wilderness for forty years.' (Acts 7:35–36)

Stephen's speech changes here from story to statements about Moses. The original Greek text uses the phrase 'this one' (*houtos*) five times in verses 35–38, underlining the point that it was this very same Moses who was sent by God as a saviour but was rejected by those he came to save. As already mentioned, Stephen has been accused of rejecting Moses, but here he spells out that, in fact, shockingly, the Israelites did just that. The parallels with what happened to Jesus are now unmistakable.

Moses was rejected (as was Jesus) despite the 'wonders and signs' he did, not only in Egypt but also for decades after in the desert. We may be tempted to assume that a church characterised by such 'wonders and signs' would pull in the punters effortlessly, but history shows that miracles do not automatically generate Christian disciples. They can certainly do so, but, as often as not, once people receive the answer to prayer that they have sought, they go on their way, perhaps without even so much as a 'thank you' to the God who has touched their lives. It happened to Jesus (Luke 17:11–19).

When we look at Jesus' ministry, we see that his primary purpose was not to be a wonderworker but to draw people into the intimate relationship with God that he himself enjoyed. Luke 8:2–3 talks of Jesus' women followers, including Mary Magdalene, being those he had healed in various ways. They received a wonderful gift but they also went on to know the giver of that gift, the source of such love and grace.

## — Reflection —

*'He came to what was his own, and his own people did not accept him. But to all who received him, who believed in his name, he gave power to become children of God'*
*(John 1:11–12).*

# The prophet to come

'This is the Moses who said to the Israelites, "God will raise up
a prophet for you from your own people as he raised me up."
He is the one who was in the congregation in the wilderness
with the angel who spoke to him at Mount Sinai, and with
our ancestors; and he received living oracles to give to us.'
(Acts 7:37–38)

Stephen continues in accusatory tones to describe the
Israelites' attitude to 'this Moses'. Here he uses a quotation
from Deuteronomy 18:15, which records Moses foretelling
the coming of another prophet, one 'raised up' as he was.
Yet again, Stephen does not in any way deny the towering
significance of Moses but emphasises how he pointed
forwards to the coming of Jesus. Also, while Moses brought
'living oracles', Jesus not only brought words of life but also,
literally, embodied the eternal life of God's kingdom.

The word translated as 'congregation' is the Greek *ecclesia*,
from which we get 'ecclesiastical' (and the French *église* and
Welsh *eglwys*). Interestingly, *ecclesia* was the usual term for the
community of Israel in the Septuagint (the Greek translation
of the Old Testament), which is what Stephen quotes. The
word did not necessarily have any particular faith-related
overtones at that time and so can serve to remind us that, in
essence, the *ecclesia*/church is a community of people rather
than a building or authority structure. Looking back at the
past with clear eyes is vital for making sense of the present
time. We may think that we know what happened 'back
then' and how events or people influenced a situation today,

but, in fact, perhaps we need to be prepared to reassess our assumptions in the light of new evidence or fresh developments.

Stephen's speech is starting to build to its climax, when his audience will be left with the excruciatingly uncomfortable message that they are the ones who are in the wrong, as their ancestors were before them. The accused is turning the tables on his accusers—a tactic unlikely to bring about a happy ending.

— Prayer —

*O God, may we not be so absorbed with what we think we know that we fail to listen to what you would teach us.*

# Rebellion

'Our ancestors were unwilling to obey [Moses]; instead, they pushed him aside, and in their hearts they turned back to Egypt, saying to Aaron, "Make gods for us who will lead the way for us; as for this Moses who led us out from the land of Egypt, we do not know what has happened to him." At that time they made a calf, offered a sacrifice to the idol, and revelled in the works of their hands.' (Acts 7:39–41)

The focus now shifts from Moses to the rebellious people, specifically the appalling incident of the golden calf (Exodus 32). They forgot that it was not simply Moses who led them from captivity but Moses acting as the obedient servant of the Lord God, hence their request to Aaron for 'gods... who will lead the way for us' (Acts 7:40). They mentally 'turned back to Egypt', yearning for the place of bitter suffering and enslavement, and literally turned their gaze away from the true God to an idol, 'the works of their hands'. In the final stage of his speech, Stephen links this theme of idolatry to the building of the temple.

It is easy to reflect on this episode with smugness, as if we would never act so stupidly. Right after the inexpressibly solemn time of covenant-making at Sinai, after the smoke, thunder and stone tablets, the Israelites smash it all to pieces. How could they?

We may ask similar questions if we see somebody we know or a figure in the media spotlight losing reputation, relationships, career or whatever as the consequence of actions that we struggle to comprehend. Susan Howatch's popular

'Starbridge' series of novels follows the tangled histories of a number of clerics whose inner turmoil leads to painful conflict with their public, professional personas. For me, the power of the novels lies in the way that she sensitively unravels the complexities of a character's heart and shows how even those in the worst messes can eventually find a path towards healing and wholeness. Even the most broken could hope for the blessing of godly wisdom, if they go in search of it.

— Prayer —

*Holy, ever-loving God, enlarge our hearts to encompass more of your mercy.*

# Relationship unravelling

'But God turned away from them and handed them over to worship the host of heaven, as it is written in the book of the prophets: "Did you offer to me slain victims and sacrifices for forty years in the wilderness, O house of Israel? No; you took along the tent of Moloch, and the star of your god Rephan, the images that you made to worship; so I will remove you beyond Babylon."' (Acts 7:42–43)

What devastating words: 'God turned away from them' (v. 42). Remember that, at this point in the narrative, we are still with the Israelites in the wilderness, when the law was given, the tabernacle made and the covenant established with all the people (rather than one individual, as in the past). This historic time of intimacy—as it were, the honeymoon of God with his chosen people—is here shown to be the point where that relationship began to unravel, leading eventually to the catastrophe of exile in Babylon. Yes, Israel offered sacrifices in the wilderness, but to the wrong gods, the 'host of heaven' (see also Jeremiah 8:2, Zephaniah 1:5).

The quote from 'the book of the prophets' is Amos 5:25–27. The Greek translators of the Septuagint struggled to understand the Hebrew language in these verses, 600 years after they were written. Nobody knows what 'Rephan' is, for example, and where Amos spoke of being removed to 'Damascus', the name was updated to 'Babylon' in the Septuagint, in the light of what actually happened. The end result was in keeping with the eighth-century BC text, while differing in some of its vocabulary.

Many churches, Christian organisations and festivals look back to a 'golden age' when every seat was taken and every ticket booked, donations flowed and vision was keen. Strangely, the 'golden age' often corresponds to the youth of those looking back! Remembering with thanksgiving is important, but being prepared to move into the future is essential, not least because the future comes, whether we are ready or not.

— Prayer —

*Faithful God, thank you for all that you have done for us in years past. Give us courage and confidence so that we can embrace all that you would do for us in years to come.*

# Listening matters

'Our ancestors had the tent of testimony in the wilderness, as God directed when he spoke to Moses, ordering him to make it according to the pattern he had seen. Our ancestors in turn brought it in with Joshua when they dispossessed the nations that God drove out before our ancestors. And it was there until the time of David, who found favour with God and asked that he might find a dwelling-place for the house of Jacob.' (Acts 7:44–46)

Having spent a while on the story of Moses, Stephen now hurries on from a tent in the wilderness to a temple. He has emphasised Moses as a forerunner of Jesus, but the temple is another matter. God had directed the making of the tent, whereas Stephen wants to show that the building of the temple was a human initiative, albeit one of David's, the heroic warrior-king 'who found favour with God'. If we are puzzled by the reference to a 'dwelling-place for the house of Jacob' (v. 46), note that a variant reading for this verse is 'for the God of Jacob'.

However close we may feel to God, however strong in faith, however insightful, we can start to assume that we know best. Instead of humbly laying out our plans in prayer and waiting patiently for assurance (whether from others or in the quiet of our own hearts), we can be convinced that we have chosen the correct course of action and may press on, only to realise afterwards that we did not start in the right place, at the right time or with the right people.

I once heard of a wealthy Western congregation that

insisted on supporting an African church leader by donating a luxurious three-piece suite for his house. The suite ended up languishing in a customs shed, due to incorrect paperwork, the soft cushions gently rotting in the tropical humidity. The urge to do something, to show compassion, concern and solidarity, was laudable, but it had to be paired with common sense and the willingness to listen—to God and also to the situation and the people concerned.

## — Reflection —

*'For wisdom is better than jewels, and all that you may desire cannot compare with her' (Proverbs 8:11).*

# Sacred space, living God

'But it was Solomon who built a house for him. Yet the Most High does not dwell in houses made by human hands; as the prophet says, "Heaven is my throne, and the earth is my footstool. What kind of house will you build for me, says the Lord, or what is the place of my rest? Did not my hand make all these things?"' (Acts 7:47–50)

Stephen was not denying that God could be found in the temple; he wanted to emphasise that the presence of God was not limited to the temple, as the quote from Isaiah (66:1–2) makes clear. The temple was a sacred space, but it was still 'made with human hands' (v. 48)—as was the golden calf. Like the golden statue, the problem lay not with the created object in itself but with the attitude of the people that subsequently developed. What should have been a means to an end (encountering the living God) became the end in itself (being custodians of the temple).

Picking up on a point made in an earlier reflection, we should remind ourselves, from time to time, that our churches are more than their buildings. Worshipping in a beautifully maintained, historic setting can be a wonderfully enriching experience, but too many congregations find the upkeep of buildings to be a major and depressing drain on their time and money. There is no doubt, though, that for arguably a majority of non-attenders, a church building says, 'This is where you can come in search of God.' The negative witness of a closed and decaying church, with an overgrown churchyard and a 'For Sale' sign outside, should not be underestimated.

There are no easy answers (there seldom are), and the missional challenge remains one of finding the balance between caring for the bricks and mortar and not becoming so devoted to their well-being that we forget that the fundamental point of the building is as a gathering place for the people.

## — Reflection —

*'How lovely is your dwelling-place, O Lord of hosts! My soul longs, indeed it faints for the courts of the Lord; my heart and my flesh sing for joy to the living God' (Psalm 84:1–2).*

# The end

'You stiff-necked people, uncircumcised in heart and ears, you are for ever opposing the Holy Spirit, just as your ancestors used to do. Which of the prophets did your ancestors not persecute? They killed those who foretold the coming of the Righteous One, and now you have become his betrayers and murderers. You are the ones that received the law as ordained by angels, and yet you have not kept it.' (Acts 7:51–53)

Finally, the speech reaches boiling point. Stephen's words are as scalding as some of Jesus' diatribes against the Pharisees (Matthew 23:16–36). Generation after generation of God's people had completely failed to recognise the Holy Spirit of God at work. They were 'uncircumcised in heart and ears' (Acts 7:51), keeping the letter of the law of Moses but not honouring the relationship that the law represented. They were blessed with the most privileged status but chose to go their own way.

Commentators stress the importance of reading Stephen's words here as part of an ongoing contemporary disagreement about the interpretation of scripture rather than in any way 'Christians attacking Jews'. The early years of the church were full of pain over the differences in understanding between the various groups, differences that finally led to permanent division. The subsequent, deeply shameful history of anti-Semitism means that such texts have to be read and preached with great care and sensitivity.

As his speech concludes, Stephen's hearers are so beside themselves with rage that they drag him away for summary execution (vv. 54–60). What is our reaction when faced with unpalatable, even harsh, truths about ourselves? Do we cover our ears and shout louder than the prophetic voice (v. 57) or do we take a deep breath and calm our angrily pounding heart to listen to what we need to hear? Perhaps, instead, we are the ones who know that we have an unpalatable truth to convey to an unwilling or even hostile audience—in which case, we can pray for the courage of one such as Stephen.

## — Prayer —

*Thank you, Lord, for the witness of your servant Stephen.*
*We commend to your care all those who face suffering*
*and even death for serving you.*

# Introduction
## Pilgrims to the cross

When the church's year comes round to Holy Week and Easter, the climax of the long weeks of Lent, the contrast with Christmas is striking. Consumer societies focus relentlessly on celebrating Christmas, with the countdown to the shopping frenzy seeming to begin earlier each time, while Easter offers a far less marketable shopping opportunity (apart from chocolate). Without Holy Week and Easter, however, Christmas is meaningless. A miraculous child was born, true, but his destiny was only fulfilled in his death and resurrection, firstfruits of a redeemed creation. Without the death and without the resurrection, we would have, at best, no more than ancient stories of an exemplary man who lived centuries ago, an inspiring character but no heaven-sent Saviour.

Our faith should find its foundation and fruition in this season, yet, too often, I myself have arrived at Good Friday unfocused, overly busy and ill prepared for the deep reflection that should characterise the days to follow.

In some ways it can be easier to immerse ourselves in the wonder of Christmas. After all, the birth of every baby seems miraculous. As a midwife once commented to me, 'I still find it amazing. One minute there are, say, four people in the room. The next, there is a new human being, taking his or her first breaths.'

Death is something that we find harder to deal with. In the case of Jesus' crucifixion, it is death as horrific public execution. It is so tempting to avert our gaze, press forward to the relief of Easter morning, overlooking the fact that, for Jesus' family and followers, this death was a catastrophe, something they had refused to countenance. Perhaps they were hoping that his sombre hints and warnings of the previous weeks were not to be taken at face value, thinking, 'How can this newly revealed Messiah, God's Anointed One, die? And die like that?'

I invite you, then, to accompany me through these readings from Mark's Gospel, which follow the way of Jesus to the cross and beyond to the astonishing empty tomb. I invite you to be a pilgrim with me, journeying in search of new understanding of the ways of our world and our God, fresh insights into the meaning and significance of what it means to live as Jesus' followers today.

# Hosanna! (Save us!)

[The disciples] brought the colt to Jesus and threw their cloaks on it; and he sat on it. Many people spread their cloaks on the road, and others spread leafy branches that they had cut in the fields. Then those who went ahead and those who followed were shouting, 'Hosanna! Blessed is the one who comes in the name of the Lord!'... Then he entered Jerusalem and went into the temple; and when he had looked around at everything, as it was already late, he went out to Bethany with the twelve. (Mark 11:7–9, 11)

The crowds press around us, pilgrims like ourselves, coming to Jerusalem for the great Passover feast. The journey may have been long and hard for many, but now the city gates are in sight and the celebratory psalm-singing begins. The noise, the jostling, the excitement grow by the moment and here is Jesus, riding an unbroken colt through the throng, an entrance carefully prepared by his followers, right down to the road carpeted in coats and branches.

It is extraordinary that the colt is not spooked by the chaos: there seem to be no fears of this rider taking an ignominious tumble. The one who calmed the wind and waves can calm a nervous animal, too. This must surely be the moment when the Messiah's public reign begins. After the years of itinerant preaching, at last all eyes will look on him with wonder and worship.

Then, however, disappointingly, he seems to behave like every other pilgrim. A quick look at the city's sights, including the all-important visit to the temple, in so many ways the centrepoint of the city, followed by what feels like a retreat to Bethany. Of course, some of his closest friends live there—Mary, Martha and Lazarus—and it is no doubt a pleasant place to stay instead of the busy streets of Jerusalem, but time is pressing for the Messiah to be revealed to the world. Surely this is no time for social calls?

## — Reflection —

*Jesus lived and breathed the purposes of God, but they did not drive out his human need for rest, recreation and companionship. Do we permit ourselves to acknowledge such needs?*

# Troublemaker

Then they came to Jerusalem. And he entered the temple and began to drive out those who were selling and those who were buying in the temple, and he overturned the tables of the money-changers and the seats of those who sold doves; and he would not allow anyone to carry anything through the temple. He was teaching and saying, 'Is it not written, "My house shall be called a house of prayer for all the nations"? But you have made it a den of robbers.' (Mark 11:15–17)

Why would Jesus never take the predictable path? Return to Jerusalem—good; return to the temple—appropriate. But now he sets about overturning the stalls that provided the necessary items for the system of sacrifices. He is outrageous enough to accuse respectable traders of being robbers. He goes so far as to stop anyone carrying anything through the temple. It is, by any reckoning, unnecessarily antagonistic.

This is a familiar story and can lose the shocking impact it would have had at the time. Imagine this disruptive energy being unleashed in a cathedral today—audio guides being knocked off the counter, Bibles grabbed from the gift shop shelves and handed to gawping visitors, and the ticket barrier (if there is one) falling to a deftly wielded crowbar. 'This is a place for praying,' shouts the vandalising (and, frankly, terrifying) figure. 'Who is praying here? Who instead is just doing their shopping or having a history lesson? You and you and you—get out! GET OUT!!'

The next verses tell us that the chief priests and scribes reacted extremely badly to this temple incident, putting Jesus on their hit list. We cannot assume that our own response would have been so different, especially if we were in some way guardians of the place under attack.

Seeing such up-ending of expectations should remind us that, while Jesus is friend, good shepherd and healer, he is also God incarnate, filled with the power that tamed chaos and brought creation to birth. We should not presume to second-guess what he would or would not approve of, but humbly listen for the prompting of his Spirit.

— Reflection —

*If Jesus visited our own place of worship, what might he challenge or even overturn?*

# Absolutely everything

He sat down opposite the treasury, and watched the crowd putting money into the treasury. Many rich people put in large sums. A poor widow came and put in two small copper coins, which are worth a penny. Then he called his disciples and said to them, 'Truly I tell you, this poor widow has put in more than all those who are contributing to the treasury. For all of them have contributed out of their abundance; but she out of her poverty has put in everything she had, all she had to live on.' (Mark 12:41–44)

If the last reading showed us a discomfiting, even threatening, Jesus, today we read of an encounter that is so moving in the tender compassion he shows towards one whose status was among the lowliest in society at that time. In recognising the true worth of the widow's offering, Jesus exemplifies the revolution that was anticipated in his own mother's song, Mary's Magnificat (Luke 1:46–55), with the needy honoured and the rich sent away empty in a divine up-ending of the usual ways of the world.

Yet we should not make the mistake of patronising this woman: 'Bless her, poor thing! What a shame for someone to be so destitute.' Such pity sees only poverty and apparent weakness when, in truth, this woman (defined according to the conventions of the time only by her marital status or, rather, lack of it) shows immense courage and cast-iron faith. Let us suppose she made her decision after due and prayerful consideration: even so, which of us would consider the option of emptying our savings account and giving it all in obedience to what we believe are God's purposes?

The consoling truth at the heart of this story is this: God notices our sacrifices. He is not distracted by the loudest voice, the flashiest credit card, the most senior rank. This woman came to the temple, humbly and unheralded, and gave everything. Jesus saw what she had done and drew others' attention to her actions. Perhaps, who knows, some of those he told about her were moved to offer her help.

— Reflection —

*Do we really believe and trust in God's provision for us?*

# In the leper's house

While he was at Bethany in the house of Simon the leper, as he sat at the table, a woman came with an alabaster jar of very costly ointment of nard, and she broke open the jar and poured the ointment on his head. But some were there who said to one another in anger, 'Why was the ointment wasted in this way? For this ointment could have been sold for more than three hundred denarii, and the money given to the poor.' And they scolded her. But Jesus said, 'Let her alone; why do you trouble her? She has performed a good service for me.' (Mark 14:3–6)

This beautiful story involves a wildly extravagant act. The precious ointment was worth nearly a year's wages. A rough estimate might set the figure at around £9000. That was the value of what was poured out on Jesus' head, yet his reaction, once again, subverts normal expectations. Sitting among those gathered in that room, we would have been overwhelmed by the fragrance of the anointing. Then we would remember the turmoil in the temple courts and Jesus' praise for the generous widow and we would probably shake our heads, baffled by this rabbi's strange value system. Whenever we think we have worked it out, everything shifts again. We love him, we follow him, but he never makes the rules clear enough. He is always one step ahead of us.

The narrative here focuses on Jesus and the woman, but we should also note the setting—the house of Simon the leper. What the Bible describes as 'leprosy' may or may not have been the mildly infectious condition also known as Hansen's disease, effective treatment for which was not developed until the 1940s. Whatever the precise diagnosis, anybody suffering from such a disease in Jesus' time (as for centuries before and after) was feared and shunned, permanently judged 'unclean'.

How does Jesus respond to Simon's situation? He accepts a dinner invitation. He relaxes, eats, drinks and socialises with the outcast and, in so doing, challenges us to do likewise.

— Reflection —

*Who are the 'outcasts' in your community? What can you and your church do to connect with them?*

# Deserted

When they had sung the hymn, they went out to the Mount of Olives. And Jesus said to them, 'You will all become deserters; for it is written, "I will strike the shepherd, and the sheep will be scattered." But after I am raised up, I will go before you to Galilee.' Peter said to him, 'Even though all become deserters, I will not.' Jesus said to him, 'Truly I tell you, this day, this very night, before the cock crows twice, you will deny me three times.' But he said vehemently, 'Even though I must die with you, I will not deny you.' And all of them said the same. (Mark 14:26–31)

When we retell the story of Gethsemane, it is tempting to focus on the betrayal by Judas, but Jesus' words here are uncompromising: 'You will all become deserters' (v. 27). Peter is included, and it can be tempting to speak disparagingly of the big fisherman, so outspoken yet so cowardly in the end. It seems unthinkable that we, too, might have abandoned Jesus, but we should be careful before confidently claiming that we would have done better had we been there that night.

The full extent of the desertion is clear if we read this passage in context. In verse 18, Jesus confronts his followers with the fact that one of them will betray him, which makes them 'distressed' (v. 19). In the verses following today's passage, Jesus withdraws with his three closest friends— Peter, James and John—who then fall asleep instead of comforting him as he agonises in prayer. Then comes the appalling conclusion: 'All of them deserted him and fled'

(v. 50) as the religious authorities and a heated crowd came to arrest him. Jesus had to face his trial alone, and the knowledge that he had foreseen this circumstance is unlikely to have been consoling.

In many churches, the altar is stripped after the Maundy Thursday Eucharist (which may include a foot-washing ceremony) and the consecrated Communion wafers are taken to a side chapel where people gather in silent meditation, remembering Jesus' lonely vigil in Gethsemane. It is a time to watch, wait and pray.

— Reflection —

*'Could you not keep awake one hour?' (Mark 14:37).*

# Dying alone

At three o'clock Jesus cried out with a loud voice, 'Eloi, Eloi, lema sabachthani?' which means 'My God, my God, why have you forsaken me?' When some of the bystanders heard it, they said, 'Listen, he is calling for Elijah.' And someone ran, filled a sponge with sour wine, put it on a stick, and gave it to him to drink, saying, 'Wait, let us see whether Elijah will come to take him down.' Then Jesus gave a loud cry and breathed his last. And the curtain of the temple was torn in two, from top to bottom. (Mark 15:34–38)

There has been darkness, three long hours of it, and, according to Mark (15:25), Jesus had already been hanging on the cross for three hours before that strange darkness fell. How long those hours will have seemed for the women, those who have loved and provided for Jesus on his travels and are 'looking on from a distance' at his dying agony (v. 40).

The cross has become such an icon of redemption that it may be startling to realise it was not adopted as such until the fifth century. Jesus was executed by a grotesque method, one designed for maximum pain and humiliation. What Mark records here sounds like misunderstanding and mockery, right to the end, as Jesus cries out the opening words of Psalm 22, words that exactly capture his physical, emotional and spiritual state. The tremendous drama of the temple curtain tearing in two takes place offstage, so that all we see here, at the Place of the Skull, is blood and death. Even the centurion's acclamation is in the past tense: 'This man *was* God's Son' (v. 39).

On Good Friday, churches hold services commemorating Christ's suffering and death. They may end in silence, the priest walking out without giving a final blessing, switching off the lights to symbolise the extinguishing of Jesus' earthly life. The congregation is left, as the first followers were, in the shadows.

— Reflection —

*When something comes to an end, we may carry on seeking signs of life, of hope, but sometimes we have to accept that we must simply grieve for what has gone.*

# A brave man

When evening had come, and since it was the day of Preparation, that is, the day before the sabbath, Joseph of Arimathea, a respected member of the council, who was also himself waiting expectantly for the kingdom of God, went boldly to Pilate and asked for the body of Jesus... Then Joseph bought a linen cloth, and taking down the body, wrapped it in the linen cloth, and laid it in a tomb that had been hewn out of the rock. He then rolled a stone against the door of the tomb. Mary Magdalene and Mary the mother of Joses saw where the body was laid. (Mark 15:42–43, 46–47)

The Jewish sabbath begins at sundown the evening before, which, as the passage states, would have been one of the reasons Joseph went to Pilate so soon after Jesus' death to request the body for burial—that and, let us surmise, the desire to remove the dead Messiah and lay him to rest, hidden from the shame and ridicule of public gaze. At least in death Jesus receives some honour, being laid in a rich man's tomb cut from the rock. Perhaps the hurry to finish all work before sundown (as the law decreed) was why the women had to return on Sunday morning, bringing the appropriate spices for anointing a corpse.

'Joses' in the passage, by the way, is a Greek form of Joseph, not a misprint for Jesus. Verse 40 identifies him as a brother of 'James the younger', who may or may not have been one of the twelve disciples.

Publicly identifying with an executed rebel (from the Romans' perspective) and blasphemer (as the Jewish authorities saw Jesus) would have demanded enormous courage from Joseph because the repercussions for such actions could have been severe and wide-ranging. As recently as 1983, when Carmen Bugan was barely in her teens, her father staged a protest against the Communist regime in Romania. Not only was he arrested and imprisoned but also the whole family suffered bitterly, as she tells in her powerful memoir *Burying the Typewriter* (Picador, 2013).

## — Reflection —

*Holy Saturday is a day for quiet reflection after the anguish of Good Friday. Then, at dusk, the Easter Vigil begins, preparing us for that most astonishing of reversals on the following day.*

# He is not here

When the sabbath was over, Mary Magdalene, and Mary
the mother of James, and Salome bought spices, so that
they might go and anoint him... They had been saying to
one another, 'Who will roll away the stone for us from the
entrance to the tomb?' When they looked up, they saw that
the stone... had already been rolled back. As they entered
the tomb, they saw a young man, dressed in a white robe,
sitting on the right side; and they were alarmed. But he said
to them, 'Do not be alarmed; you are looking for Jesus of
Nazareth, who was crucified. He has been raised; he is not
here.' (Mark 16:1, 3–6, abridged)

And so the women come 'very early' (v. 2) to complete the
burial rites, imagining, as they make their way to the tomb,
the scene awaiting them. The body will no longer be stiffened
by rigor mortis, making their work of anointing easier, but
that final act of love appears blocked by an immovable
obstacle. If that obstacle is too heavy for two women working
together, what chance for a terribly wounded young man,
revived from his coma by the coolness of the rock chamber,
trying to push from inside? Not that Jesus' followers are in
any doubt that he is dead, for surely if there had been the
tiniest sign of life left in him, they would not have sealed him
in that tomb.

In his rising, as in his living and dying, Jesus confounds
expectations once again. If we did not know the story so
well, if we were hearing it for the first time, we might find
the details verging on the hilarious, inducing incredulous

laughter along with tears of wonder. That great stone has already been rolled back; inside the tomb is no body but a mysterious young man, very much alive; the women's natural alarm is dismissed because their friend's body has somehow disappeared. This, though, is no story of a grave robbery. The one who was indisputably dead is now alive again.

— Reflection —

*The joy of Easter does not have to be a solemn joy; it can be a festive roar of delight. The impossible has happened: death has been defeated.*

# What happened next

[The young man said] 'But go, tell his disciples and Peter that he is going ahead of you to Galilee; there you will see him, just as he told you.' So [the women] went out and fled from the tomb, for terror and amazement had seized them; and they said nothing to anyone, for they were afraid. And all that had been commanded them they told briefly to those around Peter. And afterwards Jesus himself sent out through them, from east to west, the sacred and imperishable proclamation of eternal salvation.' (Mark 16:7–8)

We now reach one of the imponderables of Mark's Gospel—the ending. Nowadays, most scholars agree that the original text ended abruptly in the middle of verse 8, with the words translated as 'for they were afraid'. What we have here is the first of two alternative conclusions to the dramatic events of Easter Day, which tidy up the story to indicate that the women did do what the heavenly messenger told them to do, albeit 'briefly'. Then there is a kind of snapshot of Jesus' final commission to his followers, as told at greater length at the end of Matthew's Gospel.

The abruptness of the original ending, though, fits the abrupt narrative nature of Mark, with its vivid and rapidly changing scenes and dramatic tension. The women's reaction underlines the stupendous nature of the Easter event. 'He is dead'; 'No, he isn't'; 'So where is he?'; 'Waiting for you back in Galilee, like he promised.' It is hardly surprising that the women flee in 'terror and amazement' (v. 8): the whole situation is more than the mind can take in. As before, if we try to imagine hearing it all for the first time, the story is actually quite funny. The women do not fall to their knees and honour the heavenly messenger. Instead, they run away and say nothing.

Even if the expanded ending is textually dubious, history shows that the women must have told at least one person. The first witnesses to the staggeringly good news of the resurrection did not stay silent. Joy and faith eventually won out over their fear and confusion.

— Reflection —

*Where is Jesus? Gone ahead of us, as he always is, waiting for us to follow.*

# What else happened next

Now after he rose early on the first day of the week, he appeared first to Mary Magdalene, from whom he had cast out seven demons. She went out and told those who had been with him, while they were mourning and weeping. But when they heard that he was alive and had been seen by her, they would not believe it. After this he appeared in another form to two of them, as they were walking into the country. And they went back and told the rest, but they did not believe them. (Mark 16:9–13)

This and the next two readings cover passages from the second alternative conclusion to Mark's Gospel (see the previous reading for more on the alternative endings). Based on a high incidence of vocabulary not found elsewhere in Mark's Gospel, plus strong parallels with post-resurrection accounts in Matthew, Luke and John, as well as Acts, scholars now surmise that this section was not part of the original text.

It is interesting, though, to read these verses for the somewhat different light they shed on those early days of Easter. In telling the story, we may tend (naturally enough) to conflate the four Gospels and forget how each writer shaped the material to bring out particular truths and emphases. We can move, Hollywood-style, from John's radiant dawn meeting between Jesus and Mary Magdalene in the garden to Luke's vivid Emmaus road scene to Matthew's hilltop farewell tableau, and forget to read each account on its own terms, noting what is included and omitted.

Even if the status of these final verses is doubtful, they are still in tune with Mark's overall emphasis on exploring how people respond to Jesus, both the Saviour himself and his teaching. Here we have the radiant John scene and the vivid Luke scene almost deflated by the disbelief of those hearing the reports of what has happened. The good news is treated as a tall tale, a wish-fulfilment fantasy brought on by the stress of bereavement. The saying goes that 'if something is too good to be true, it usually is'. But not where the kingdom of heaven is concerned.

## — Reflection —

*How open are we to being astonished by God?*

# Rebuked

Later he appeared to the eleven themselves as they were sitting at the table; and he upbraided them for their lack of faith and stubbornness, because they had not believed those who saw him after he had risen. And he said to them, 'Go into all the world and proclaim the good news to the whole creation. The one who believes and is baptised will be saved; but the one who does not believe will be condemned.' (Mark 16:14–16)

The abrupt, bubble-puncturing tone of this alternative ending continues. John's Gospel presents us with Jesus bestowing peace and the Holy Spirit on his frightened friends (20:19–22), reassuring the doubter (vv. 27–29), and serving breakfast in that wonderful beach episode (21:1–23). Luke provides equal measures of reassurance and explanation (24:36–49). Here, Jesus sounds almost brusque, a tone of voice found in other passages in Mark, such as the cursing of the fig tree (11:12–14), fruitless simply because it was not the season for figs.

Such brusqueness is, surely, what we also hear in the voice of God, confronted yet again by the stubborn rebellion of his people, even as they wandered in the wilderness after the exodus, dependent on heavenly food and heavenly guidance. We hear it in the anger of the prophets as their divinely inspired warnings fall unheeded. We see it across the Gospels as Jesus turns on the religious leaders who are failing in their duty of care for the people. God has, since the very beginning, loved humanity, longed for them to listen and lamented their turning away.

We may find the final words in this passage very uncomfortable. Indeed, 'condemned' sounds horrifyingly harsh, but if the Son of God brings salvation, then whoever does not accept the Son of God cannot receive that salvation. This is a logical consequence, not punishment. What is not spelled out here, though, is the timescale for such condemnation—and we have an infinite God, with infinite love and infinite patience. That is the context for such uncomfortable words.

## − Reflection −

*Jesus says, too, that they are to preach 'to the whole creation'.*
*What might be good news for the non-human parts*
*of creation?*

# Wonder-working

[Jesus said] 'And these signs will accompany those who believe: by using my name they will cast out demons; they will speak in new tongues; they will pick up snakes in their hands, and if they drink any deadly thing, it will not hurt them; they will lay their hands on the sick, and they will recover.' So then the Lord Jesus, after he had spoken to them, was taken up into heaven and sat down at the right hand of God. And they went out and proclaimed the good news everywhere, while the Lord worked with them and confirmed the message by the signs that accompanied it. (Mark 16:17–20)

Many of the 'signs' listed here by Jesus are found in the book of Acts, including Paul's encounter with a poisonous snake after his shipwreck (28:3–5). Commentators are at pains to point out that Jesus is not condoning such behaviour—as if downing a pint of poison is a valid way of demonstrating God's power and protection. Having said that, a relatively small number of Pentecostal-style churches in the USA claim inspiration from these verses to include snake-handling and drinking strychnine in their worship services, with occasionally (and unsurprisingly) fatal results.

Whatever our preferred style of worship, we should seek signs of God at work in our community, in the wider world and in our own lives. We would be as mistaken to deny that God can act miraculously here and now as we would be to base our faith entirely on signs of the more spectacular kind. Of course the eternal, omnipotent Lord of space and time can heal, for example, but we should never assume that healing is somehow less holy because it comes about through modern medical expertise, rather than being drug-free and instantaneous.

The point is not the sign in itself, however headline-grabbing it might be, but the faith generated by a combination of gospel message shared and heavenly grace received.

## — Reflection —

*Jesus' followers are sent out into a hostile world, with the reminder that the power of God's kingdom surrounds and sustains them as they go—as we are still sent and as we are still surrounded and sustained.*

# — Part 3 —

## In resurrection light

Suddenly we are out in the daylight, blinking perhaps, but finding solid ground beneath our feet, blue skies above. The darkness is past, the confusion is over (for now, anyway) and we find our hearts strengthened with the assurance that the one who raised Jesus from the dead can raise us to new life, too. And he does not just raise us to life but blesses us with sufficient strength and clarity of vision to continue to do his work in the world.

In this final section of readings, we consider the good shepherd, who leads us so gently on the right paths; we reflect on gardens found in scripture, places that can restore the soul but may still (human nature being what it is) end up being a cause of sorrow; we ponder the power of God's Spirit—breath of life and blazing fire—who acts decisively to transform the world.

As the following poem hints, we are known by name; we are loved more than we can ever know; we are called by Father, Son and Spirit to walk on in the light of the resurrection, the weight of sin lifted from our shoulders, discovering more and more of the healing that is freely extended to all God's children. Realistically, we acknowledge that hard times will almost certainly come round again, but joyfully we affirm that the risen Jesus is with us, as past experience strengthens our faith that bit more to help us face with fortitude whatever tomorrow may bring.

# Walking with God

Eyes open—
A voice half-heard by the heart
Asleep,
Calling your real name.

Morning rises all around,
Shining with presence.
Wind rushes through the grass—
Up and over the hill—
Follow,
And breathe,
Breathe so deep
And feel life
Running right
To your soul's core.

# Introduction
## The Good Shepherd

A while ago, a kind nun explained to me what it meant to have a 'special devotion' (in faith terms). I had sometimes wondered about the significance of the titles common in the Roman Catholic Church—what it meant for nuns to describe themselves as 'Sister Margaret [or whoever] of the Holy Cross' or 'of the Sacred Heart'. My friend told me that such titles signified the 'special devotion' of the nun concerned— that is, an aspect of Christian belief or an episode or character in the Gospel story that most inspired her faith and prayers.

Intrigued by this, I began to wonder what my 'special devotion' might be. As a long-standing employee of The Bible Reading Fellowship, surely the Bible would be the most appropriate response in my case? What about God the Father, or Mary the mother of Jesus, seeing as I have written a fair bit about parenting, the love of God and related ideas?

Then, as I prayed one day, it came to me: the Good Shepherd. Of course! As far back as I can remember, I have loved stories and pictures inspired by the biblical idea of God as shepherd, caring for us, his flock. When I was very small, my mother would sing me to sleep with a Victorian bedtime prayer: 'Jesus, tender shepherd, hear me/Bless your little lamb tonight.' Psalm 23 was the first psalm I ever learned and is still one of my favourites. Still, reflecting on the patience, gentle care and security symbolised by the Good Shepherd remains a rich source of consolation and inspiration for me.

In the following readings, we will reflect on some of the Good Shepherd passages from the Old and New Testaments.

These include some famously lovely words, but they can become overly familiar if we forget their wider context and read them purely to apply to ourselves. We should not forget, either, that being a shepherd was, and often still is, a solitary, arduous and occasionally dangerous job. Both sheep and shepherd are vulnerable, and they need each other.

A final thought: as you read, you may find the Good Shepherd to be a particularly meaningful image for you, too. If not, you could try prayerfully to identify your own 'special devotion'.

# He is with us

The Lord is my shepherd, I shall not want. He makes me lie down in green pastures; he leads me beside still waters; he restores my soul. He leads me in right paths for his name's sake. Even though I walk through the darkest valley, I fear no evil; for you are with me; your rod and your staff—they comfort me. You prepare a table before me in the presence of my enemies; you anoint my head with oil; my cup overflows. Surely goodness and mercy shall follow me all the days of my life, and I shall dwell in the house of the Lord my whole life long. (Psalm 23)

We begin with the quintessential Good Shepherd passage— best beloved of all the psalms, offering as it does the deepest reassurance that the Lord (YHWH in the original Hebrew, the mysterious and unpronounceable name of God) is with us. His presence sustains us, no matter what has happened, no matter where we are. The psalm begins and ends with reflection on God's loving care, while the imagery shifts from shepherd and sheep to guest and host at a lavish dinner party.

It is worth noting that while the psalm is tagged as being 'of David', some commentators interpret 'the house of the Lord' as referring to the temple, which was built after David's time. The temple was significant not only as the place of sacrifice and public and private prayer but also as the very visible symbol, in the middle of the city, of God's presence with his people.

At the heart of this psalm is the sobering thought that, despite the shepherd's care, dark and dangerous places are unavoidable. The bad news is that, however well-behaved and careful we are, we will end up journeying through them at some point, because that is life and sometimes life is very hard. The good news is that, even in the most fearful circumstances, we are assured that we have a heavenly armed guard alongside us.

— Reflection —

*Take time to read through Psalm 23 aloud, phrase by phrase, and wait in silence to hear God's gentle whisper in your heart.*

# He cherishes us

Get you up to a high mountain, O Zion, herald of good tidings; lift up your voice with strength, O Jerusalem, herald of good tidings, lift it up, do not fear; say to the cities of Judah, 'Here is your God!' See, the Lord God comes with might, and his arm rules for him; his reward is with him, and his recompense before him. He will feed his flock like a shepherd; he will gather the lambs in his arms, and carry them in his bosom, and gently lead the mother sheep. (Isaiah 40:9–11)

These verses are from the turning-point in the book of Isaiah, where judgement and despair turn to comfort and hope. The whole of Isaiah 40 is a profoundly poetic meditation on the grandeur and majesty of God, but here we find a wonderful juxtaposition of images—the coming of the mighty king who is also the gentle shepherd. We will reflect more in the next reading on the traditional connection between those two images in the culture of that time; here let us meditate on the tenderness of the one who picks up his lambs and cuddles them.

Depending on our personal experiences of being loved and looked after, we may or may not find it easy to imagine being held in a safe and secure embrace. Whatever our experiences, we may find it harder still to imagine that such intimacy can characterise our relationship with God. Yes, as Isaiah 40 tells us, God is sovereign, eternal, 'the Creator of the ends of the earth' (v. 28); yet, at the same time, he cherishes us with a love more enduring than that of any mother (49:15).

If we know we have neglected our relationship with God,

we may end up so racked with guilt that we cannot bear to open our Bibles, let alone pray. We may endure times so storm-tossed that we feel too damaged even to think about whether or not our faith can help us. That is when we can hold on to the knowledge that the Good Shepherd promises to hold us, carry us, cuddle us.

— Reflection —

*'Do not fear, for I am with you, do not be afraid, for I am your God' (Isaiah 41:10).*

# He cares for us

For thus says the Lord God: I myself will search for my sheep, and will seek them out. As shepherds seek out their flocks when they are among their scattered sheep, so I will seek out my sheep. I will rescue them from all the places to which they have been scattered on a day of clouds and thick darkness. I will bring them out from the peoples and gather them from the countries, and will bring them into their own land; and I will feed them on the mountains of Israel, by the watercourses, and in all the inhabited parts of the land. I will feed them with good pasture, and the mountain heights of Israel shall be their pasture; there they shall lie down in good grazing land, and they shall feed on rich pasture on the mountains of Israel. I myself will be the shepherd of my sheep, and I will make them lie down, says the Lord God. (Ezekiel 34:11–15)

The dramatic book of Ezekiel is not as well known as it ought to be but it is a particular favourite of mine (not least for its spellbindingly strange imagery in places). I find this passage a beautiful evocation of God's care.

In the ancient Near East, as far back as the third millennium BC, shepherding was used as an image for the task of governing people. Here, the Lord God is being the Good Shepherd, in contrast to the bad shepherds (kings) who have woefully failed to look after Israel. As a result of their failure, the people have been violently dispersed, exiled, far from the land of milk and honey. They have been lost, but now the Good Shepherd will bring them home and nurse them back to health.

This passage shows us that God cares not just for individuals but also for whole nations. We may rightly emphasise the importance of cultivating our individual relationship with the shepherd, but what about the relationship between the shepherd and our family, our community, our church, our country?

## — Reflection —

*The Lord is my shepherd; the Lord is our shepherd; the Lord is your shepherd.*

# He searches for us

Now all the tax-collectors and sinners were coming near to listen to him. And the Pharisees and the scribes were grumbling and saying, 'This fellow welcomes sinners and eats with them.' So he told them this parable: 'Which one of you, having a hundred sheep and losing one of them, does not leave the ninety-nine in the wilderness and go after the one that is lost until he finds it? When he has found it, he lays it on his shoulders and rejoices. And when he comes home, he calls together his friends and neighbours, saying to them, 'Rejoice with me, for I have found my sheep that was lost.' Just so, I tell you, there will be more joy in heaven over one sinner who repents than over ninety-nine righteous persons who need no repentance.' (Luke 15:1–7)

The opening words of this reading are a useful reminder that Jesus' teaching was not delivered in the first-century equivalent of the Sunday morning 'sermon slot', but out on the road, in the middle of everyday life and the heat of the day, surrounded by jostling crowds and irritated opponents.

The parable of the lost sheep is the first in a series of three such stories that focus on how Jesus' way was to connect with the 'sinners' whom the religious hierarchy wanted to exclude. His way meant connecting not in order to condemn but to welcome them and enjoy their company.

If, like me, you first encountered this story as a children's picture book, you may, like me, have thought of it as being primarily about the misadventures of a bad sheep who wilfully went astray. We may, as a result, find it surprising to rediscover that the real point is not the waywardness of the sheep but the tenacity of the shepherd. He is even ready to risk the entire flock (left not in a safe fold but 'in the wilderness') for the sake of the missing one. After the sheep has been found, there is communal rejoicing—and all this for the sake of one single sheep.

— Reflection —

*Do we believe that we matter that much to the shepherd?*
*Do we believe that those we find easy to label 'sinners'*
*matter that much to him, too?*

# He dies for us

'I am the good shepherd. The good shepherd lays down his life for the sheep. The hired hand, who is not the shepherd and does not own the sheep, sees the wolf coming and leaves the sheep and runs away—and the wolf snatches them and scatters them. The hired hand runs away because a hired hand does not care for the sheep.' (John 10:11–13)

We must not forget how shocking Jesus' words would have sounded to their original audience. He is applying to himself imagery used by the prophets to refer to the Lord God. Rather than telling a story about a hypothetical good shepherd, he is here explicitly identifying himself as that shepherd, the true Good Shepherd of Israel.

This teaching follows the story of the healing of the man born blind, who was then rejected by the Pharisees (John 9). Together they point to the fact that the religious leaders were conspicuously failing in their pastoral duty of care for the people. The identity of the 'hired hand' who 'runs away' (v. 12)—in contrast to the good shepherd—would therefore have been all too obvious to Jesus' listeners.

The good shepherd, Jesus says, is even willing to risk his own life to save his sheep from wild animals. These days, and in heavily urbanised countries, the threat of approaching wolves can sound more like a fairytale scenario than the harsh reality it would have been in New Testament times. Thinking about it, the hired hand's response sounds quite reasonable. After all, how prepared would we be to die to save an animal, even a favourite pet?

In this, we see that the love of the Good Shepherd for us, his sheep, is breathtaking in scope, beyond reason, extended to every one of us, whether we feel safe in the fold or straying, lost or found. It has the quality of selflessness that is the hallmark of true love, where nothing matters more to the lover than the well-being of the beloved and where love is lavished, whether or not a response is forthcoming.

## — Reflection —

*The perfect sacrifice looks away from self towards the other, largely unaware that there is any sacrifice.*

George Guiver et al., *Priests in a People's Church* (SPCK, 2001)

# He knows all of us

'I am the good shepherd. I know my own and my own know me, just as the Father knows me and I know the Father. And I lay down my life for the sheep. I have other sheep that do not belong to this fold. I must bring them also, and they will listen to my voice. So there will be one flock, one shepherd.' (John 10:14–16)

I like the joke about heaven where Peter is showing round a newcomer and they pass a closed door, from behind which singing can be heard. 'Who's in there?' asks the newcomer. 'Oh,' says Peter, 'that's the [insert denomination of choice]. They think they're the only ones here.'

Following on directly from our previous reading, our passage repeats and extends Jesus' words about his identity as the Good Shepherd. It is also a further rebuke to the listening Pharisees, who were obsessed with maintaining the 'purity' of 'their' flock and excluding the 'other'—in this case, the Gentiles. As with the response of the hired hand, the attitude is: why should a hardworking shepherd expend effort on somebody else's flock? This, though, is yet another reminder of the scandalous generosity of God's love: it is really and truly limitless. There are no favourites, no hierarchies, no first and second class. Everybody is welcome.

Jealousy is one of the earliest emotions we know, especially if we have siblings close in age to us. We love to be loved, but it can be hard to accept that others have a right to share that love. The good news is that not only is God's love inexhaustible but also, as we are touched by his love, we begin to be changed and learn to love as he does. His love can enlarge the smallness of our hearts and the narrowness of our understanding of his grace.

— Reflection —

*The Lord Jesus was sent to tell us that we are loved and that God has called us into the same intimacy that he shares with the Father and the Spirit. Caught up in that love we, too, are sent to love as we have been loved.*

Jean Marie Dwyer OP, *The Sacred Place of Prayer* (BRF, 2013)

# As we follow his example

I exhort the elders among you to tend the flock of God that is in your charge, exercising the oversight, not under compulsion but willingly, as God would have you do it—not for sordid gain but eagerly. Do not lord it over those in your charge, but be examples to the flock. And when the chief shepherd appears, you will win the crown of glory that never fades away. (1 Peter 5:1b–4)

As I mentioned in the Introduction, shepherd and sheep need one another. The flock needs the shepherd's care, and it is hard for the shepherd to be a shepherd without a flock to care for. Acknowledgement of this mutual dependence should (so today's Bible passage tells us) be at the heart of the relationship between church leaders and members. Rather than pursuing high office, wide influence or lots of adulation, a godly leader must focus their ambition on being a faithful and obedient servant. Of course, ministry work must be carried out competently and managed efficiently, but the primary aim must always be nurturing the well-being of the flock and not enhancing the status of the shepherd. Any 'crown of glory' comes from God alone, at the end of all things.

In the Anglican ordination service, the bishop tells those about to be ordained that they should always be mindful of the example of the Good Shepherd as they pursue their calling. These are not just generally inspiring words, but an essential part of mission. If church leaders fulfil their duty of demonstrating the love and care of the Good Shepherd to their people, in their turn the people will be enabled to demonstrate that love and care to one another and the wider world. As that happens, the world can look at the church (the body of Christ, 1 Corinthians 12:27) and glimpse a little of what God is like. That is why it is important to pray as often as we can for those who lead our churches and also for those who lead the leaders.

— Reflection —

*May it one day be said of you, not necessarily that you talked about God cleverly, but that you made God real to people.*
Michael Ramsey, *The Christian Priest Today* (SPCK, 2009)

# Introduction
## Gardens and God

Wandering the back streets of a southern Mediterranean or north African city, you may find yourself passing a high stone wall. If you do, look up: you may be rewarded by a glimpse of lush greenery just climbing over the top and perhaps hear the faint sound of falling water coming from a hidden garden. The locked garden squares found in central London also offer tantalising glimpses of escape from city pavements into a realm of verdant lawns and manicured rose beds—but only for those privileged enough to be key-holders.

In so many countries, the secluded, well-tended garden is synonymous with living the good life. It is a place to relax, enjoy yourself and create an atmosphere of beauty and harmony (even if you employ somebody else to do the literal dirty work). In a dry and dusty land, abundance of water and vegetation are particular luxuries and it is hardly surprising that when we turn to the Bible, we find a variety of well-watered gardens described—both actual places and metaphors for the spiritual state of an individual or people.

In these readings, we will consider some of the gardens described in the Bible, ranging from groves of trees outside Jerusalem to Eden, the original garden paradise. It is a helpful reminder that the story of creation is not only about us—men and women, called to 'fill the earth and subdue it' (Genesis 1:28). Before we came along on the sixth day, God had been at work shaping the cosmos, every single bit of which he judged to be 'good'. Just as we are described as being made in God's image (v. 26), so we can learn something of God not only from each other but also by looking at the work of his hands (in accordance with the reasoning known as 'natural theology').

Whether or not the season of harvest is at hand as we follow these readings, the imperative of thankfulness remains. God has blessed us with a beautiful world and given us the task of making it more beautiful. We can and should thank him for the fertility of the earth that provides not only food for the body but also food for the soul.

# Paradise remembered

And the Lord God planted a garden in Eden, in the east; and there he put the man whom he had formed. Out of the ground the Lord God made to grow every tree that is pleasant to the sight and good for food, the tree of life also in the midst of the garden, and the tree of the knowledge of good and evil. A river flows out of Eden to water the garden... The Lord God took the man and put him in the garden of Eden to till it and keep it. And the Lord God commanded the man, 'You may freely eat of every tree of the garden; but of the tree of the knowledge of good and evil you shall not eat, for in the day that you eat of it you shall die.' (Genesis 2:8–10a, 15–17)

When thinking of Eden, it is easy to imagine a kind of stately home splendour—all herbaceous borders and clipped yews, with Adam toiling away alongside his wheelbarrow. If we focus on what the Bible passage actually says, we notice that Eden sounds more like an oasis. God provides a 'garden' of fruiting trees with an abundant water supply; it is up to the man to 'till it and keep it' (v. 15).

Notice that the text uses 'Lord God' (vv. 8, 15), combining the covenant name YHWH, disclosed to Moses, with 'Elohim', the name for God in Genesis 1. Here, God is recognised both as creator and as covenant partner with the human race. The creator/covenant-making one, in his care for humanity, does not simply provide a suitable home and profitable work to do but also creates conditions: 'You may freely eat... you shall not eat' (vv. 16–17).

Why should gaining knowledge about good and evil lead

to death? A moment of reflection on the state of the world shows that knowledge exercised without wisdom can lead to immense suffering. We must accept our limitations, our human frailty, and ask for God's help before we can hope to begin to live wisely and use our knowledge well.

## − Reflection −

*We cannot begin the journey away from fragmentation*
*towards wholeness until we accept our own*
*and the world's woundedness.*
Ray Simpson, *Hilda of Whitby* (BRF, 2014)

# The garden of love

A garden locked is my sister, my bride, a garden locked, a fountain sealed. Your channel is an orchard of pomegranates with all choicest fruits, henna with nard, nard and saffron, calamus and cinnamon, with all trees of frankincense, myrrh and aloes, with all chief spices—a garden fountain, a well of living water, and flowing streams from Lebanon.

Awake, O north wind, and come, O south wind! Blow upon my garden that its fragrance may be wafted abroad. Let my beloved come to his garden, and eat its choicest fruits. (Song of Songs 4:12–16)

Here is another paradisaical garden, overflowing with sensory and sensual delight. The lover is expounding the beauty of his bride, listing a bewildering array of scented plants and fruits to evoke quite how lovely she is. The NRSV notes, delicately, 'meaning of Hebrew uncertain' for the word translated 'channel', so I will leave it to you to ponder what the lover may have been talking about.

Like Eden, this garden has an ample water supply, with a well that constantly bubbles up, fresh and 'living', even though the fountain is 'sealed'. There are further reminders of Eden in the mention of 'choice fruits', but, in this garden of bliss, eating these fruits means celebrating love and life, not embarking on a path leading to loss and pain, as did the man and woman in Eden.

This is also a 'garden locked': the woman will release herself only for her lover, who will give himself to her alone (2:16; 6:3; 7:10, although mention of 'Solomon' elsewhere brings to mind the very different and far less balanced relationships between kings and harems). Just as a dam holds back water so that it can be released safely, so, within the boundaries of faithfulness and commitment, deep love and desire can be safely expressed. Within these boundaries, such love can be channelled for nurturing, as well as delighting, another, rather than simply employed to satisfy our own appetites.

## — Reflection —

*We need to understand and control our passions, for through them we can recognise and release the divine self-giving love of creation.*

Andrew Clitherow, *Desire, Love and the Rule of St Benedict* (SPCK, 2008)

# Land grab

Naboth the Jezreelite had a vineyard in Jezreel, beside the palace of King Ahab of Samaria. And Ahab said to Naboth, 'Give me your vineyard, so that I may have it for a vegetable garden... I will give you a better vineyard for it; or, if it seems good to you, I will give you its value in money.' But Naboth said to Ahab, 'The Lord forbid that I should give you my ancestral inheritance.' Ahab went home resentful and sullen... He lay down on his bed, turned away his face, and would not eat... As soon as Ahab heard that Naboth was dead, Ahab set out to go down to the vineyard of Naboth the Jezreelite, to take possession of it. (1 Kings 21:1–4, 16, abridged)

I recall years of driving along the A40 in London, past rows of boarded-up semis purchased for a road-widening scheme that never happened. The gardens of the empty houses ran wild, with only the occasional shrub or tree serving as a reminder of their former owners' care by continuing to bud each spring.

The 'compulsory purchase' in this passage is a blatant land grab, an extreme example of power abused. Naboth pays with his life for protecting his ancestral piece of ground (v. 13) from the predatory king. The land (the promised land) was God's gift to his people—the foundation of the covenant, along with the law that showed them how they should live. Land was to be considered as held in trust for the Lord God (Leviticus 25:23) rather than treated as a disposable commodity.

I find it impossible to reflect on this story without being

reminded of present-day issues of territory and possession in the Holy Land, a region that, we should remember, is sacred to Christians, Jews and Muslims. In our response to such a complex and immensely painful situation as we see there today, we should resist the temptation to give quick answers and reflect instead on the wider message of scripture—that we are called to work for justice, peace and care for all.

## — Reflection —

*'They shall all sit under their own vines and under their own fig trees, and no one shall make them afraid; for the mouth of the Lord of hosts has spoken' (Micah 4:4).*

# Fruitless labour

My beloved had a vineyard on a very fertile hill. He dug it and cleared it of stones, and planted it with choice vines; he built a watch-tower in the midst of it, and hewed out a wine vat in it; he expected it to yield grapes, but it yielded wild grapes... And now I will tell you what I will do to my vineyard. I will remove its hedge, and it shall be devoured; I will break down its wall, and it shall be trampled down... and it shall be overgrown with briers and thorns; I will also command the clouds that they rain no rain upon it. For the vineyard of the Lord of hosts is the house of Israel, and the people of Judah are his pleasant planting; he expected justice, but saw bloodshed; righteousness, but heard a cry! (Isaiah 5:1–2, 5–7, abridged)

It looked so promising—fertile soil, good situation, choice plants, a hardworking gardener—but the toil, expense and patience did not pay off. Instead of the anticipated abundance, the 'beloved' (an echo of the Song of Songs, perhaps) ends up with a useless crop of small, sour fruit. His disappointment and anger are graphically described—and then comes the prophet's punchline. What he is speaking about are the nations of Israel and Judah.

The story reveals both the extent of God's loving care in tending his 'vineyard' and the extent of his anger when that care does not yield a harvest. To drive home the point that this is wilful, rather than involuntary, fruitlessness, we have the contrast (involving wordplay in the original Hebrew) of bloodshed instead of justice, a crying out instead of righteousness.

Jesus uses similar imagery in the parable of the tenants (found in Matthew, Mark and Luke) and in John 15:1: 'I am the true vine, and my Father is the vine-grower.' Biblical teaching reflects clearly the life and times of the people to whom it was originally addressed, drawing illustrations from what was to be seen and experienced all around. If we preach and teach the Bible, it is good to bear this in mind.

## — Reflection —

*'Those who abide in me and I in them bear much fruit, because apart from me you can do nothing' (John 15:5).*

# Betrayal in the garden

[Jesus] went out with his disciples across the Kidron valley to a place where there was a garden, which he and his disciples entered. Now Judas, who betrayed him, also knew the place, because Jesus often met there with his disciples. So Judas brought a detachment of soldiers together with police from the chief priests and the Pharisees, and they came there with lanterns and torches and weapons. Then Jesus, knowing all that was to happen to him, came forward and asked them, 'For whom are you looking?' They answered, 'Jesus of Nazareth.' Jesus replied, 'I am he.' Judas, who betrayed him, was standing with them. (John 18:1–5)

I once talked to a travel writer who spoke of how his faith had grown as a result of visiting Israel. Although he already knew, of course, that the events of Jesus' life took place in a real landscape, which can still be visited today, he had not reckoned on the powerful spiritual impact of actually walking in those places.

There are four contenders for the site that John names as the garden where Jesus spent the night before his betrayal (it is called 'Gethsemane', Aramaic for 'oil press', only in the Gospels of Matthew and Mark). Even so, the visitor can get a sense of what the garden would have looked like. A grove of olive trees rather than our preconceived notion of flowers and shrubs, it would still have been a place of pleasant shade where, John tells us, Jesus would 'often' meet with his disciples.

John's Gospel is known for its layers of meaning and the

richness of its imagery. We should not feel we are being too fanciful, then, if we detect echoes here of God walking in Eden, with the man and the woman he had made. Back then, as in our passage today, the garden was a place of struggle between good and evil, a place of betrayal, of the darkness seeming to defeat the light.

As we will see in our next reading, though, it is in another of John's gardens that we witness the light triumphing over the darkness, once and for all.

— Reflection —

*'The light shines in the darkness, and the darkness
did not overcome it' (John 1:5).*

# Garden burial

Joseph of Arimathea, who was a disciple of Jesus, though a
secret one... asked Pilate to let him take away the body of
Jesus... Nicodemus, who had at first come to Jesus by night,
also came, bringing a mixture of myrrh and aloes, weighing
about a hundred pounds. They took the body of Jesus and
wrapped it with the spices in linen cloths, according to the
burial custom of the Jews. Now there was a garden in the
place where he was crucified, and in the garden there was
a new tomb in which no one had ever been laid. And so,
because it was the Jewish day of Preparation, and the tomb
was nearby, they laid Jesus there. (John 19:38–42, abridged)

Although Jesus is buried stealthily, by two secret disciples,
it is still a kingly burial. He is accorded the honour of being
the first to be laid in a newly made tomb, his body dressed
with a huge quantity of spices, presumably as pungent as any
evoked in the poetry of the Song of Songs.

The scene is one that, in its very familiarity, can lose
its emotional power, but we can reread the passage now,
lingering over the twice-used phrase 'the body of Jesus'. Two
men tend the corpse of one who, when living, healed the
sick with no more than a word and raised the dead. Joseph
and Nicodemus, reverently folding the battered limbs of their
rabbi and friend in linen cloths, will surely remember such
scenes and struggle to understand, yet again, how things can
have come to such a terrible end.

The wonder of this garden is to be revealed in a matter of
hours, for it is the place where the miracle of resurrection

will have the last word, instead of the despair of death. On Easter morning, Mary Magdalene comes, looks through her tears and mistakes the risen Jesus for the gardener—which, in a way, he is, just like his Father.

## — Reflection —

*Now the green blade riseth from the buried grain,*
*Wheat that in dark earth many days has lain;*
*Love lives again, that with the dead has been:*
*Love is come again, like wheat that springeth green.*

John Crum (1928)

# Harvesting the fruits of the garden

The time is surely coming, says the Lord, when the one who ploughs shall overtake the one who reaps, and the treader of grapes the one who sows the seed; the mountains shall drip sweet wine, and all the hills shall flow with it. I will restore the fortunes of my people Israel, and they shall rebuild the ruined cities and inhabit them; they shall plant vineyards and drink their wine, and they shall make gardens and eat their fruit. I will plant them upon their land, and they shall never again be plucked up out of the land that I have given them, says the Lord your God. (Amos 9:13–15)

Ruins rebuilt, in a land dripping with wine (it was once described as 'flowing with milk and honey', Exodus 3:8) and so fertile that the harvest is still being gathered as the new crops are planted. Unlike Isaiah's 'beloved', with his failed vineyard, the people will literally enjoy the fruit of their labours—and no enemy will steal it from them.

What we see here is not only the promise of restoration after exile, but an undoing of the consequences of the fall, when years of sweat and toil would produce no more than the bare essentials of life, amid a lot of 'thorns and thistles' (Genesis 3:17–19). Without going as far as full-on prosperity theology, on the basis of this and many other Bible passages we can safely say that God wants the best for his people. He made a good and beautiful world to delight his earth-creatures. When they rejected relationship and chose their own selfish ways, again and again and again, they reaped the bitter consequences.

Here, though, the Lord himself declares that he will overturn those consequences. He wants to set everything to rights, the way it was meant to be, from the beginning. That is the hope in which we, too, live. Whatever our failures, our wounds, our self-inflicted catastrophes, the Lord God is in the business of making good. He will, one day, fix us, and our lives will bear good fruit.

## — Reflection —

*God never ever tires of forgiving us. It is we who tire of asking for forgiveness.*

From Pope Francis' first *Angelus*, St Peter's Square
(17 March 2013)

# Introduction
## The valley of dry bones: Ezekiel

The vision of the valley of dry bones is one of those Bible passages whose fame eclipses its original context. It inspired the traditional spiritual song 'Dem Bones' (anatomy and scripture lesson combined), as well as providing a haunting image for those seeking to bring words of Christian encouragement to a difficult situation.

The book of Ezekiel (where this vision falls, in chapter 37) is not as widely read or quoted as (say) Isaiah. Interestingly, however, biblical studies lecturer Ernest Lucas describes Ezekiel as 'one of the most visual of the major Hebrew prophets in the presentation of his message... Some of the other prophets occasionally perform symbolic actions, but Ezekiel performs what amounts to "street theatre"' (*The People's Bible Commentary: Ezekiel*, BRF, 2002). At times, the prophet literally acts out his message (such as the siege of Jerusalem in chapter 4), and the dry bones vision is one of a number that involve him being what we might call 'teleported' to a particular location where God wishes to speak to him. This includes the rather painful note of his being carried to Jerusalem by 'a lock of my head' (8:3)!

The context for Ezekiel's ministry was the exile. A quick reminder: after the death of Solomon, Israel split into the kingdom of Israel, with its capital Samaria, and Judah, centred on Jerusalem. The two kingdoms faced the perennial problems associated with being small states surrounded by superpowers. Israel was defeated by the Assyrian empire in 722/1BC, and Judah was finally overwhelmed by the

Babylonians in 587/6 BC. Defeat meant hordes of people being taken into captivity abroad and the devastation of their city.

The dry bones episode comes in the final section of Ezekiel (chs. 33—48), which brings messages of hope and restoration after many earlier oracles of warning and judgement. These messages culminate in a breathtaking vision of a restored Jerusalem, the very name of which will be 'The Lord is There' (48:35). It would seem that, even as news of the fall of the first Jerusalem reached the captives (33:21), God spoke to assure them that all was not lost. And the final reading in this section, from the book of Daniel, indicates the right response to such assurance.

# Dried up

The hand of the Lord came upon me, and he brought me out by the spirit of the Lord and set me down in the middle of a valley; it was full of bones. He led me all round them; there were very many lying in the valley, and they were very dry. (Ezekiel 37:1–2)

One of the things I love about mid-Wales is the hidden valleys. Driving through the countryside (or cycling if I am feeling energetic), I take a side turning and a whole new landscape unfolds, hidden from the main road by the green hills, with its own settlements, woods and water. The valley described in the passage today could not be more different from those landscapes. The impression is of a gulch, a deep valley formed by erosion that, if the eroding river is dried up, can be prone to flash floods. It sounds a dried-up, hostile, isolated place.

In this silent gulch—too deep for the wind to do more than whisper, far from any human habitation—the prophet's feet tread in among heaps of bones. Led by the 'spirit of the Lord', he walks through what looks like the site of a terrible battle or perhaps a massacre of unarmed civilians. Whatever it was, it happened so long ago that not only has all the clothing rotted away but also the very bones have been bleached completely dry.

Some would argue that any place where devastating loss of life has occurred, especially if it involved betrayal or summary execution, retains a chilling atmosphere. Think, they would say, of Glencoe, Wounded Knee, Auschwitz or Nyarubuye.

Miraculously, however, life does go on even after terrible atrocities. Survivors slowly and painfully pick up the pieces of their lives and begin the long journey towards some kind of normality. Ezekiel's valley, however, is empty of everything except the remains of the dead: there were no survivors to bury the bodies, mourn them and pay them due respect. There appears to be no hope of healing or any kind of restoration.

## — Reflection —

*Pause to remember before God those who have died in wars, whether in direct combat or as victims of 'collateral damage'. Remember, too, those who did not die but whose lives were scarred by those deaths.*

# God knows how

He said to me, 'Mortal, can these bones live?' I answered, 'O Lord God, you know.' Then he said to me, 'Prophesy to these bones, and say to them: O dry bones, hear the word of the Lord. Thus says the Lord God to these bones: I will cause breath to enter you, and you shall live. I will lay sinews on you, and will cause flesh to come upon you, and cover you with skin, and put breath in you, and you shall live; and you shall know that I am the Lord.' (Ezekiel 37:3–6)

From the first moment of Ezekiel's calling to be a prophet, when he saw 'the appearance of the likeness of the glory of the Lord' (1:28), he was subjected to a series of disturbing visions and supernatural encounters, whereby he received words from God for the exiled people. After the very public humiliation of enacting the siege of Jerusalem (an ordeal that cost him more than 14 months) and the orders to shave his hair and beard and eat an admittedly tasty scroll, he is now called upon to prophesy to dried-up bones in an eerie valley. At least nobody is watching…

To the Lord's challenge—'Can these bones live?'—the prophet makes a wise response. The obvious answer is, 'No, of course not', but Ezekiel is loyal to his faith in the one God, mightier than any foreign deity, whose power is not limited by territorial considerations.

We may face a situation—in our personal lives, at work, in our church—that seems insurmountably difficult. We may have taken a step in what we thought was obedience to God, only to find that everything appears to be unravelling and what we had thought was a right choice seems to be turning out to be a fatal error. In such situations, the wise course is to be like Ezekiel here and hold on to what we know of God, trusting that if we continue to seek his way and follow his command, life will come even from death.

## — Reflection —

*'Then Job answered the Lord: "I know that you can do all things, and that no purpose of yours can be thwarted"'*
*(Job 42:1–2).*

# Seriously, can these bones live?

So I prophesied as I had been commanded; and as I prophesied, suddenly there was a noise, a rattling, and the bones came together, bone to its bone. I looked, and there were sinews on them, and flesh had come upon them, and skin had covered them; but there was no breath in them. (Ezekiel 37:7–8)

Obediently, Ezekiel speaks to the bones, telling them that the Lord Almighty will restore them to life, against every appearance to the contrary. Then comes that wonderfully dramatic word—'suddenly'—and the drama of the scene intensifies. First comes the noise, a rattling, and we imagine the prophet breaking off, scared out of his wits, looking this way and that as the source of the noise becomes apparent. The bones are moving. As the prophet watches (I think, open-mouthed), the bones are reconstituted into bodies. First, the sinews knit the bones together, then the flesh covers them and, finally, the skin grows over all and they are recognisably human bodies rather than human remains. They are still dead, though.

Does Ezekiel panic at this point? The first words of prophecy that the Lord had given him for these wretched bones, as we read yesterday, were 'I will cause breath to enter you, and you shall live.' He has prophesied and, lo, the job of resurrection is only half done. Again, the drama deepens, for does this then show that the Lord is not, in fact, quite so powerful after all?

This passage is a reminder that even if something looks

good, it can still lack the breath of life. In Welsh, the word for 'spirit'/'Spirit' is *ysbryd*, while *ysbrydoliaeth* means 'inspiration'. Without the life-giving inspiration of the Spirit of God, our work, our relationships or our worship can feel as hopeless as somebody moving the limbs of a dead body and then shouting, 'Look! They're still alive!' In truth, there is no life and only an illusion that life could be possible, for, even if there is a body, how can breath return to that which drew its last breath many, many years before?

— Reflection —

*'The spirit of God has made me, and the breath of the Almighty gives me life' (Job 33:4).*

# Gift and giver

Then he said to me, 'Prophesy to the breath, prophesy, mortal, and say to the breath: Thus says the Lord God: Come from the four winds, O breath, and breathe upon these slain, that they may live.' I prophesied as he commanded me, and the breath came into them, and they lived, and stood on their feet, a vast multitude. (Ezekiel 37:9–10)

There is a wonderfully creepy engraving of this scene by the French artist Gustave Doré. It shows the prophet standing at a relatively safe distance, silhouetted by apocalyptic clouds as the skeletons literally pull themselves together and get to their feet.

Following on from our Welsh lesson (the language of heaven, or so I am told), we can note that the Hebrew word *ruach* is used for three different English words in the passage here—'breath', 'wind' and 'spirit'—making these verses rich with layers of meaning. The same word occurs in Genesis 1, when 'a wind from God' (NRSV) or 'the Spirit of God' (NIV) sweeps over the dark, pre-creation waters, and in Genesis 2:7, where God breathes into the man 'the breath of life'.

We may be tempted to envisage a kind of zombie army here, silently staring at the anxious prophet as he wonders what on earth will happen next. The dead are alive, however, not just undead, and they are a 'vast multitude'. The desolate gulch would surely now fill with noise. Perhaps there are shouts of recognition, astonished laughter and also tears as the newly resurrected multitude mingle among the rocks.

We might wonder, too, whether God provided clothing as well as breath!

While the Bible is no science textbook, it is absolutely clear that God is the life-giver for all. Whatever the exact mechanism by which the gift was first given, the source of it is the Lord Almighty, who is also our heavenly Father. It is a gift that is terribly easy to take for granted until we find we risk losing it—or fear its loss for one we love. Today, let us recollect both gift and giver and give thanks.

## — Reflection —

*'How precious is your steadfast love, O God! ... For with you is the fountain of life' (Psalm 36:7, 9).*

# He has heard them

Then he said to me, 'Mortal, these bones are the whole house of Israel. They say, "Our bones are dried up, and our hope is lost; we are cut off completely."' (Ezekiel 37:11)

Finally we come to the point of this prophecy, but, as Ernest Lucas points out, it has often been misunderstood: 'From early Christian times, both Christian and rabbinical commentators have tended to read it in terms of the bodily resurrection' (*PBC Ezekiel*). In fact, at that time, there was no concept of life after death. All the dead, righteous and unrighteous alike, were thought to end up in a shadowy region known as Sheol. While Ezekiel's vision is a reminder that the Lord is the giver of life, it is also intended to teach that life can come from death in a metaphorical, rather than literal, sense.

The 'whole house of Israel' feels itself dried up and dead; hope is gone. As mentioned in the Introduction to these notes, God's people had suffered the fate common to so many smaller countries that have the misfortune to be surrounded by empires. Both Israel and Judah were fought over, dominated and eventually swallowed up, once they had wilfully distanced themselves from God's protection. Now they no longer dare even ask for divine help because they have been 'cut off completely', not only from the temple (the heart of their worshipping life) but from the promised land, which was the centrepiece of the covenant. God, however, is bigger than they thought (as the next reading will show). He has heard their despairing cries and will respond beyond expectation.

While few places manage to avoid conquest altogether, it is salutary to reflect on the fate of, for example, some Central European countries that have repeatedly found themselves the victims of conflicting major powers. Such troubled history can have an impact on a people's sense of identity and self-worth that can continue, for better or worse, down the centuries. While many of the exiles from Israel and Judah were eventually able to return home, the trauma of exile changed things for ever.

— Reflection and prayer —

*Pray for refugees, those who work with them and anyone who feels, for whatever reason, exiled from home.*

# Up from the grave

'Therefore prophesy, and say to them, Thus says the Lord God: I am going to open your graves, and bring you up from your graves, O my people; and I will bring you back to the land of Israel. And you shall know that I am the Lord, when I open your graves, and bring you up from your graves, O my people. I will put my spirit within you, and you shall live, and I will place you on your own soil; then you shall know that I, the Lord, have spoken and will act, says the Lord.' (Ezekiel 37:12–14)

Now the Lord gives Ezekiel his orders: 'Tell my people that I am coming for them.' They may be metaphorically dead and buried, but God will show that that is no obstacle to his plans. Just as dry bones can become living beings again, so God's people can and will be resurrected.

The imagery here is quite different from and far more moving than that in yesterday's passage. Instead of the grotesque rattling of reassembling skeletons, we can imagine somebody uncovering a mass grave. As the bodies are uncovered, they are gently lifted and placed beneath the sky. The one digging lays aside the shovel and leans over the bodies, one by one, and breathes on them. Then, because this breath is the breath of life, the dead, one by one, stir and snatch a lungful of air. Their eyes open and, behold, they are alive again.

The promise to God's people is not only of resurrection but also of restoration to their own land. The English translation does not show that the same Hebrew word, *adam* (yes, as in the Adam of Genesis), is used here for both the 'land' of Israel and 'soil'. This is a homecoming that involves reconnecting with a place once known intimately—the kind of knowledge that farmers and devout gardeners have.

God has spoken; God will act. What the people have to do is trust, and wait for the word to be fulfilled.

## — Reflection —

*'And the ransomed of the Lord shall return, and come to Zion with singing; everlasting joy shall be upon their heads; they shall obtain joy and gladness, and sorrow and sighing shall flee away' (Isaiah 35:10).*

# The right response

[Daniel prayed] 'Now therefore, O our God, listen to the prayer of your servant and to his supplication, and for your own sake, Lord, let your face shine upon your desolated sanctuary. Incline your ear, O my God, and hear. Open your eyes and look at our desolation and the city that bears your name. We do not present our supplication before you on the ground of our righteousness, but on the ground of your great mercies. O Lord, hear; O Lord, forgive; O Lord, listen and act and do not delay! For your own sake, O my God, because your city and your people bear your name!' (Daniel 9:17–19)

Daniel's prayer (9:4–19) is made 'in the first year of Darius… who became king over the realm of the Chaldeans' (v. 1). He has calculated that the 70 years allotted for 'the devastation of Jerusalem' (v. 2) are finished. It must therefore be time for the restoration foreseen by Ezekiel, among many other prophets. Even so, this prayer is made 'with fasting and sackcloth and ashes' (v. 3) and consists largely of repentance for the people's sins. Daniel understands all too well the unfaithfulness of Israel and Judah, but he also knows how unfathomable is the faithfulness of God.

God makes the first move to mend the broken relationship, but that does not absolve the people of responsibility. They must be mindful of his mercy and respond with due humility, even as the promises of return come closer to fulfilment. When they are back on their own soil, will they raise a 'harvest of righteousness' (James 3:18) or not?

While we can never deserve the grace that is lavished on

us from heaven, we should not be tempted to take it lightly either. God's desire is to see us transformed into the people he always intended us to be, fully fit for his purposes. That transformation is unlikely to be a quick, easy or painless process. Even so, I think we can safely assume that the prize will be worth the process.

## — Reflection —

*'A new heart I will give you... and I will remove from your body the heart of stone and give you a heart of flesh'* (Ezekiel 36:26).

# Introduction
## Holy fire

These readings on 'holy fire' were originally written for early January, one of the coldest, darkest times of year. It's the time when the festive atmosphere of Christmas has faded away, even if we have kept the decorations up until Epiphany. While your personal January may be cheered by a birthday or similar celebration, it can feel like a long and weary progression of days until the first hint of spring.

If we are used to the wall-to-wall warmth of central heating and the ease of flicking a switch to flood a room with light, it can be hard to appreciate the importance of a fire on a cold morning or a candle on a dark night. My family and I sometimes stay at a cottage where there is no heat until you kindle the woodstove and the limited electricity supply comes from a small wind generator. After a day or so, both light and heat are appreciated as the precious resources that they really are.

We should remember that when we read Bible passages about 'light', the words were written many centuries before the invention of electric light. That means, as far as the original audience was concerned (and for generations after), 'light' and 'fire' came to the same thing—a living flame, whether an oil lamp, a manageable blaze on a hearth or a catastrophic inferno.

In these readings, we will reflect on passages from across scripture to do with fire and light to see what they can teach us about our faith and God. We will ponder the manifestation of the Lord as mysterious fire in the desert and the Holy Spirit appearing as flame and wind at Pentecost. We will think about how fire is presented as both purifying and destructive and wrestle with the implications of the 'fires of judgement'.

Along the way, we will consider two special days in the church calendar, both of which have associations with light and fire—Candlemas (also known as the Presentation of Christ in the Temple), which falls on 2 February, and 1 February, when we remember Brigid of Kildare.

# Something like

As I looked, a stormy wind came out of the north: a great
cloud with brightness around it and fire flashing forth
continually... In the middle of it was something like four living
creatures... Over the heads of the living creatures there was
something like a dome, shining like crystal... And above the
dome over their heads there was something like a throne,
in appearance like sapphire; and seated above the likeness
of a throne was something that seemed like a human form.
Upward from what appeared like the loins I saw something
like gleaming amber, something that looked like fire enclosed
all round... This was the appearance of the likeness of the
glory of the Lord. (Ezekiel 1:4–5, 22, 26–28, abridged)

This astonishing vision is probably less well-known than
Isaiah's experience, but it is an equally bold attempt to
express the inexpressible. Do take a moment at some point
to read the whole chapter and imagine your response if a
friend or relative returned from a stroll by the river with such
a tale to tell!

We do not have space to explore the possible significance
of the four living creatures, the crystal dome, the sapphire
throne and so on. What we can appreciate here, though, is
the dazzling poetic imagery and the way it establishes the
theme of God's sovereignty, which pervades the book of
Ezekiel. There are representations of many kinds of animal,
all-seeing eyes, the mention of a rainbow (that ancient
symbol of hope), and God enthroned above all.

Ezekiel's vision came while he was among the Jewish

exiles in Babylon and unequivocally demonstrates that the Lord is God of the entire cosmos. The chosen people are far from the temple, but not far from God—and the power of the Almighty is not in any way diminished by a foreign context. Although the tremendous glory of the Lord is heightened by contrasting it with the people's sinfulness, Ezekiel's message is ultimately one of hope and restoration and the unstoppable power of heaven.

## — Reflection —

*Note how the prophet carefully states that 'this was the appearance of the likeness of the glory of the Lord', rather than declaring boldly 'I saw God'. Let's maintain a similar humility when we share our experiences of God with others.*

# Fire in the wilderness

[The Israelites] set out from Succoth, and camped at Etham, on the edge of the wilderness. The Lord went in front of them in a pillar of cloud by day, to lead them along the way, and in a pillar of fire by night, to give them light, so that they might travel by day and by night. Neither the pillar of cloud by day nor the pillar of fire by night left its place in front of the people. (Exodus 13:20–22)

The phrase 'a pillar of cloud' conjures up images of a tornado—that fearful twisting spiral reaching down from thunderous clouds to wreak havoc where it touches down. This cloud, however, was a guiding presence, a way of indicating a path through pathless places, and, at night, perhaps its fiery appearance was warming and protective for the people as well.

Anybody who has ever camped in the wild will know how comforting a fire can be, even if they are not camping in a place where there are predators large and fierce enough to fancy them for a midnight snack. Firelight means companionship, a measure of comfort and the possibility of food. Mountaineer Joe Simpson's book *Touching the Void* (Vintage, 1988) describes his agonising solitary journey to safety after a terrible fall and tells of his anguish at crawling, after nightfall, over the final ridge before base camp—only to see no sign of light beyond. For a desolate few hours, he assumed that his companions had given up hope and left him (fortunately, they had not).

Whatever our favoured brand of churchmanship, we can

gain solace and inspiration from physical reminders of God's protecting and consoling presence in our places of worship, whether in the form of a simple cross, a beautifully painted icon or the sanctuary light burning to indicate that the reserved sacrament is housed nearby. We may feel that it is preferable to believe in our hearts that God is with us and that he loves us, but sometimes even superheroes of faith can benefit from an outward sign of otherwise intangible grace.

## — Reflection —

*'The Lord is your keeper; the Lord is your shade at your right hand. The sun shall not strike you by day, nor the moon by night' (Psalm 121:5–6).*

# Chariot of fire

When they had crossed [the Jordan], Elijah said to Elisha, 'Tell me what I may do for you, before I am taken from you.' Elisha said, 'Please let me inherit a double share of your spirit.' He responded, 'You have asked a hard thing; yet, if you see me as I am being taken from you, it will be granted you; if not, it will not.' As they continued walking and talking, a chariot of fire and horses of fire separated the two of them, and Elijah ascended in a whirlwind into heaven. Elisha kept watching and crying out, 'Father, father! The chariots of Israel and its horsemen!' But when he could no longer see him, he grasped his own clothes and tore them in two pieces. (2 Kings 2:9–12)

What a way to go! Probably not most people's choice when envisaging their preferred death, though. It sounds like an episode from the TV series *Lost*, where plane crash survivors on a remote island contended with an increasingly bizarre plotline involving time travel, monsters and mysticism. I wonder how Elijah felt as he made that final, dizzying ascent? Would he have been terrified or exhilarated by the astonishing light?

Another example of somebody being 'taken' by God is Enoch (Genesis 5:21–24). Hebrews 11:5 explains that this happened because he had 'pleased God' and cites him as a hero of salvation history. Similarly, Elijah's end befits his enduring status in both Jewish and Christian thought. Indeed, traditionally, an empty seat is still kept at the Passover table in case he returns.

Although forewarned that his master was leaving (and

despite the divine honour implicit in the manner of his leaving), Elisha is distraught. Commentators cannot agree on the meaning of his incoherent cry as he watches, but he shows his sorrow by tearing his clothes. Even the hope of the promised 'double portion' of Elijah's prophetic gift does not stop him grieving. Envisaging our loved ones in the glory of the Lord's presence does not stop us longing for them to be with us again. That is not wrong; it is simply human.

## — Reflection —

*Elijah experienced God as both heavenly fire and a gentle whisper. Let us be open to however God chooses to reveal himself to us.*

# This great sight

Moses was keeping the flock of his father-in-law Jethro, the priest of Midian; he led his flock beyond the wilderness, and came to Horeb, the mountain of God. There the angel of the Lord appeared to him in a flame of fire out of a bush; he looked, and the bush was blazing, yet it was not consumed. Then Moses said, 'I must turn aside and look at this great sight, and see why the bush is not burned up.' When the Lord saw that he had turned aside to see, God called to him out of the bush, 'Moses, Moses!' And he said, 'Here I am.' Then he said, 'Come no closer! Remove the sandals from your feet, for the place on which you are standing is holy ground.' (Exodus 3:1–5)

This divine encounter is no huge storm of light and fire, but a phenomenon intriguing enough to catch Moses' attention. What if he had ignored it? God's sovereign purposes would not have been thwarted by a man too lacking in curiosity or scared to draw close, but subsequent events might have unfolded differently.

Are we inclined always to hurry on by and never 'turn aside'? Although life is often unavoidably busy, we may risk missing a transformative encounter more often than we know.

Moses was a fugitive, washed up in the wilderness because he had tried to act the hero and use his adopted Egyptian status to save a fellow Hebrew but ended up as a murderer instead (Exodus 2:11–15). Now, because he is prepared to 'turn aside', his circumstances are turned upside down. The

God of his true fathers, Abraham, Isaac and Jacob (3:6), the God who has done great things in the past, will act again.

God's calling to Moses proved to be an extraordinarily difficult one, bringing suffering not only to himself but also his wider family. Sometimes he must have recalled this desert encounter as a reminder that his life was not his own: he had given himself in obedience to the Lord Almighty.

## — Reflection —

*Moses had to remove his shoes because he was on holy ground, standing in God's presence. Followers of a number of world faiths still do the same before worship; how should Christians acknowledge God's presence?*

# The splendour of his majesty

In the year that King Uzziah died, I saw the Lord sitting on a throne, high and lofty; and the hem of his robe filled the temple... The pivots on the thresholds shook at the voices of [the seraphs] who called, and the house filled with smoke. And I said: 'Woe is me! I am lost, for I am a man of unclean lips, and I live among a people of unclean lips; yet my eyes have seen the King, the Lord of hosts!' Then one of the seraphs flew to me, holding a live coal that had been taken from the altar with a pair of tongs. The seraph touched my mouth with it and said: 'Now that this has touched your lips, your guilt has departed and your sin is blotted out.' (Isaiah 6:1, 4–7)

This prophetic calling is one of the best-known in scripture. It shares many similarities with Ezekiel's experience and with some descriptions in the book of Revelation (4:3–11, for example). A modern-day writer attempting to express what was seen and heard might perhaps use strobe lighting, throbbing bass guitar lines and hallucinogenic colours.

In this passage, we find the theme of purging fire, something we will consider in later readings. For now, we will focus on Isaiah's response to finding himself surrounded by the light of heaven. He does not need to be told that he is 'unclean': in the presence of the Lord of hosts, he knows that he is as unworthy of love and mercy as the most cynical and sinful of the people. The brighter the light, the clearer we see the grime and flaws, whether in our surroundings or in ourselves.

Reassuringly, no sooner has Isaiah acknowledged his guilt than the coal plucked from the altar burns away his guilt. The seraph, servant of God, tells him that his sin is not only forgiven but also 'blotted out', utterly cleansed. The prophet is now prepared to serve the Lord.

## — Reflection —

*Imagine yourself in the shadowless brightness of God's gaze. Is there anything that you would rather keep hidden? Realise the futility of such a hope and ask for mercy, knowing that God is more than willing to grant it.*

# Blazing Spirit

When the day of Pentecost had come, they were all together in one place. And suddenly from heaven there came a sound like the rush of a violent wind, and it filled the entire house where they were sitting. Divided tongues, as of fire, appeared among them, and a tongue rested on each of them. All of them were filled with the Holy Spirit and began to speak in other languages, as the Spirit gave them ability. (Acts 2:1–4)

Pentecost fell on the 50th day after the sabbath of Passover week, originally celebrated as the harvest festival and later linked to a commemoration of the giving of the law on Sinai. A highly symbolic occasion, then, for this dramatic moment of wind and fire that took place seven weeks after Jesus' death and ten days after his ascension, as the pattern of the Christian calendar still reminds us.

'They', referred to in the passage, were not just the eleven remaining apostles (following the loss of Judas) plus their new recruit, Matthias, but the wider circle of Jesus' followers. This group had continued to meet together, waiting and hoping for the coming of the Spirit that their Master had promised before his bodily presence left them (Acts 1:8). Now, at Pentecost, that promise would be fulfilled and the next phase in the spreading of the gospel message would begin. The harvest would ultimately be global, but also personally costly for many of those gathered in that house.

The small tongues of flame were a sign of God's presence coming to indwell each one of the disciples. It was not so much that everyone had their own personal 'bit of God', but they were drawn into the one great blaze of the Spirit. All had been cleansed from sin, for ever, through Jesus' atoning death, so all could be drawn into the Spirit's work of testifying to what God had done through his Son.

## — Reflection —

*The gift of 'other languages' (here meaning other human languages, not* glossolalia, *also known as 'speaking in tongues') was bestowed for a specific and weighty purpose. Jesus' followers were to share the good news with the crowds gathered in the city, rather than stay indoors and enjoy a private worship session.*

# Refiner's fire

See, I am sending my messenger to prepare the way before me, and the Lord whom you seek will suddenly come to his temple... But who can endure the day of his coming, and who can stand when he appears? For he is like a refiner's fire and like fullers' soap; he will sit as a refiner and purifier of silver, and he will purify the descendants of Levi and refine them like gold and silver, until they present offerings to the Lord in righteousness. Then the offering of Judah and Jerusalem will be pleasing to the Lord as in the days of old and as in former years. (Malachi 3:1–4, abridged)

As well as offering warmth and light, as well as being beautiful and at times terrifying to behold, fire can be used to cleanse. Our passage speaks of 'the day of his coming'—the 'day of the Lord' mentioned again and again in the scriptures as the time when God will come in power to right every wrong. Even the 'descendants of Levi', the priestly tribe, are not exempt from the refiner's fire: leaders, as well as the people, must be made clean in order to be 'pleasing to the Lord'.

The refining imagery here is linked to two industrial processes—washing woollen cloth and heating metal to remove impurities. In both processes, the result is a useful and valuable product, one made fit for purpose. One of the key innovations of 19th-century Britain was the Bessemer process, enabling the mass-production of malleable steel from a brittle form of iron and so vastly expanding the scope of the Industrial Revolution.

Such processes always involve stress, hard work and the

expenditure of physical and mental energy. They are not easy, but the end result is worth it. Our tendency is to assume that 'if it hurts, it must be bad for us', yet God does not apply the 'refiner's fire' or 'fullers' soap' for sadistic ends. What he does need to do, though, is cleanse and shape his children so that they are readied for his holy and eternal purposes.

## − Reflection −

*Dare we ask God to refine us and refine our churches until we are fit for purpose?*

# Burned clean

'Even now the axe is lying at the root of the trees; every tree therefore that does not bear good fruit is cut down and thrown into the fire. I baptise you with water for repentance, but one who is more powerful than I is coming after me; I am not worthy to carry his sandals. He will baptise you with the Holy Spirit and fire. His winnowing-fork is in his hand, and he will clear his threshing-floor and will gather his wheat into the granary; but the chaff he will burn with unquenchable fire.'
(Matthew 3:10–12)

These verses come from one of John the Baptist's famously fiery speeches. Addressing members of two of the leading faith groups of the day, who had come for baptism (v. 7), he denounces them as a 'brood of vipers' and adds for good measure that God could create children of the covenant from the stones underfoot (v. 9). Despite their social status, the religious leaders are far from beyond reproach. John then describes the one 'coming after' him, who will bring a new baptism of Spirit and fire. To explain what he will be like, he evokes a farmer hard at work, flexing his muscles to swing his axe and clear the dead wood, sifting chaff from grain and burning the waste until not a trace is left.

We may find these words uncomfortable because we struggle to relate them to ourselves or to those we know and love. Should we be trembling lest the celestial farmer judge us (or them) as useless and throw us into the unquenchable fire like a pile of old sticks?

It is important to remember that the burning branches

are not being punished; they are being tidied away, as today we shred and compost garden waste. The farmer is making the field fit for purpose (an echo of the previous reflection). Rather than worrying that we might be 'dead wood', we should reflect on the 'chaff' in our lives that needs to be discarded—the wrong attitudes, unhelpful habits and the cobwebbed corners that we hide from God's love and grace.

## — Reflection —

*'I am the vine, you are the branches. Those who abide in me and I in them bear much fruit, because apart from me you can do nothing' (John 15:5).*

# Lake of fire

> Then I saw a great white throne and the one who sat on it; the earth and heaven fled from his presence... And I saw the dead, great and small, standing before the throne, and books were opened. Also another book was opened, the book of life. And the dead were judged according to their works, as recorded in the books... Then Death and Hades were thrown into the lake of fire. This is the second death, the lake of fire; and anyone whose name was not found written in the book of life was thrown into the lake of fire. (Revelation 20:11–12, 14–15, abridged)

This is one of those passages over which people have argued for centuries, so we cannot hope to tie up the loose ends here! That said, there are two issues to bear in mind. First, Revelation should not be read in a woodenly literalistic way. It is an apocalypse, a dramatic genre, using vivid imagery to present spiritual truths. A good commentary or well-trained preacher is an essential aid to understanding it.

Second, we should not confuse these verses with verses 9–10, where the hellish enemies of God are 'tormented day and night for ever and ever' in the fiery lake. According to one well-respected view, our passage indicates that, while eternal life is the reward of the faithful, the rest are simply annihilated, ceasing to exist for ever, in a 'second death'. Note, too, that the dead are judged 'according to their works', rather than according to their faith. Perhaps (whisper it) God cares more about how we lead our lives than the correctness of our doctrine.

As we reflect on these huge matters, we must hold on to what scripture tells us—that God loves the world so much, he sent his one and only Son to save every single one of us. Salvation is a gift freely available to all who choose to receive it.

## — Reflection —

*To have a hell of torment, with no remission or hope of repentance, is to have God sustaining, in his perfect new creation, a part of it which will always be in rebellion against him, and which can only be described as evil.*

Marcus Maxwell, *The People's Bible Commentary: Revelation* (BRF, 2005), p. 195

# Perpetual fire

The Lord spoke to Moses, saying: Command Aaron and his sons, saying: This is the ritual of the burnt-offering. The burnt-offering itself shall remain on the hearth upon the altar all night until the morning, while the fire on the altar shall be kept burning. The priest shall put on his linen vestments… and he shall take up the ashes to which the fire has reduced the burnt-offering on the altar, and place them beside the altar… A perpetual fire shall be kept burning on the altar; it shall not go out. (Leviticus 6:8–10, 13, abridged)

On 1 February the church calendar commemorates Brigid of Kildare (c.454–525), renowned for establishing religious communities in Ireland after being inspired by Patrick's preaching. The most famous of these communities was for both men and women at Kildare and offered hospitality, education and worship. Stories tell that her pagan father named Brigid after the Celtic fire goddess and, interestingly, when she came to Kildare, she decided to maintain the ancient, pre-Christian 'perpetual fire' there, choosing to 'rebrand' it as the light of Christ. That fire may have burned right up to the 16th-century suppression of the monasteries, but was then not rekindled until 1993. It is now tended by the Brigidine Sisters, a restoration of Brigid's original monastic order.

Brigid's reinterpretation of the pagan fire as Christian was an approach, in many ways, typical of Celtic spirituality. Instead of labouring to remove every vestige of the old ways, the tendency was to absorb and redirect the best of them into a Christian worldview. Thus, people came to realise that the beliefs and powers they held as sacred were not, in themselves, evil but merely inadequate—just a vague intimation of the true Lord of creation.

It is interesting to realise how a 'perpetual fire' was part of the worship ritual ordained by God for the Israelites. The fire of sacrifice purified the people by consuming the offerings that they brought to symbolise their sin, so its continuing to burn was a powerful sign that God's purifying work never comes to an end.

## — Reflection —

*What are the 'old ways' of our culture that we can redirect so that they honour the Lord God?*

# The light of the world

Now there was a man in Jerusalem whose name was Simeon; this man was righteous and devout... and the Holy Spirit rested on him. It had been revealed to him by the Holy Spirit that he would not see death before he had seen the Lord's Messiah. Guided by the Spirit, Simeon came into the temple; and when the parents brought in the child Jesus... Simeon took him in his arms and praised God, saying: 'Master, now you are dismissing your servant in peace, according to your word; for my eyes have seen your salvation, which you have prepared in the presence of all peoples, a light for revelation to the Gentiles and for glory to your people Israel.' (Luke 2:25–32, abridged)

Candlemas (2 February) is the day when the church remembers Jesus' parents bringing him to the temple to be 'presented to the Lord' as the law prescribed for a firstborn male (v. 23) and for Mary's ritual purification, 40 days after the birth. Those relatively routine events were, however, an occasion for yet another reminder of Jesus' extraordinary destiny. Not only was there the prophetic meeting with Simeon, but an elderly woman, the prophet Anna, also approached and proclaimed the baby as a sign of hope 'to all who were looking for the redemption of Jerusalem' (v. 38).

This day is known as Candlemas because it is traditionally the day when church candles for use over the coming year are blessed. In pre-Christian times, a festival of light took place at this time, marking the midpoint between the shortest day and the spring equinox (and so the midpoint of winter).

What better way to redeem this ancient and understandable impulse than to link it to remembering the Christ-light breaking into the world?

Candlemas marks a turning point in the church calendar, when the focus shifts from 'after Christmas' to 'before Easter'. The words that Simeon goes on to speak to Mary are soberingly prescient: her child will be 'a sign that will be opposed' and, ominously, her own soul will be pierced as with a sword (vv. 34–35). The brighter the light, the sharper the shadows.

— Reflection —

*'The light shines in the darkness, and the darkness did not overcome it' (John 1:5).*

# Letting the light shine

[Jesus said] 'No one after lighting a lamp hides it under a jar, or puts it under a bed, but puts it on a lampstand, so that those who enter may see the light. For nothing is hidden that will not be disclosed, nor is anything secret that will not become known and come to light. Then pay attention to how you listen; for to those who have, more will be given; and from those who do not have, even what they seem to have will be taken away.' (Luke 8:16–18)

In the Introduction to these readings, I mentioned how a few days away from the National Grid is a good reminder of the value of light. There is effort involved in pouring out lamp oil, trimming a wick and ensuring protection from draughts; and—as Jesus humorously points out—you do not go to all that trouble only to hide the light under a bed.

The point of light (obviously) is to provide illumination, not only for ourselves but also for those who enter the lit room. Equally, the light of the gospel that we believe as Jesus' followers not only illuminates our lives but also draws others to it. It reveals the true nature of whatever we bring into the light, whether good or bad, strong or weak, useful or a hindrance.

In today's world, where we try to avoid accusations of 'unfairness' at all costs, the final verse sounds troubling. The context is not, however, a crudely literal 'God helps those who help themselves'. We should think instead of Jesus' parable of the talents (Matthew 25:14–30), with its model of working with the 'master' who bestows gifts in order to multiply them, whether great or small. We have the gift of salvation in order to spread the good news of God's kingdom; it is not for our personal gratification alone. We should be careful how we listen, then, so that we do not allow the truth merely to wash over us but allow it to take root within our hearts.

## — Reflection —

*Is there a danger that praying for 'revival fire to sweep the land' can actually be a way of dodging the hard work of personally lifting up the gospel light in our homes and communities?*

# Lakeside barbecue

When [the disciples] had gone ashore, they saw a charcoal
fire there, with fish on it, and bread. Jesus said to them, 'Bring
some of the fish that you have just caught.' So Simon Peter
went aboard and hauled the net ashore, full of large fish, a
hundred and fifty-three of them; and though there were so
many, the net was not torn. Jesus said to them, 'Come and
have breakfast.' Now none of the disciples dared to ask him,
'Who are you?' because they knew it was the Lord. Jesus came
and took the bread and gave it to them, and did the same
with the fish. (John 21:9–13)

This passage is rich in the deeper meanings and echoes of
earlier episodes characteristic of John's Gospel. Richard A.
Burridge (in *The People's Bible Commentary: John*, BRF, 1998)
points out that the Greek word for the charcoal fire is used
in only one other place—for the fire in the courtyard where
Peter betrayed Jesus (18:18)—while the word for the fish
cooking on the fire means the same sort of dried fish as in
the feeding of the 5000 (6:9–11). The precise number of the
fish has also taxed the ingenuity of commentators over many
centuries.

While it is rewarding to explore a passage in such depth,
it is still good to read it as a narrative, albeit one so startling
in its juxtaposition of divine and mundane. Here is the risen
Jesus, a matter of weeks after the world-shattering events of
the first Easter, and he is hosting a barbecue on the beach.
The ordinary is hallowed, filled with powerful symbolism,
by the presence of the Son of God, yet he also affirms the

goodness of the ordinary by his actions. This is not magic fish or miraculous bread, but the everyday snack food of that culture. Equally, Jesus does not hold a prayer meeting or preach to his friends but simply shares a meal with them, as he would have done so often in the past. As then, times of such loving fellowship offer more than enough opportunity for the Spirit to move among us.

## — Reflection —

*If you are preparing a meal today, pause and think of Jesus being present with you, blessing the work of your hands.*

# The blaze of glory

> Then I turned to see whose voice it was that spoke to me, and on turning I saw seven golden lampstands, and in the midst of the lampstands I saw one like the Son of Man, clothed with a long robe and with a golden sash across his chest. His head and his hair were white as white wool, white as snow; his eyes were like a flame of fire, his feet were like burnished bronze, refined as in a furnace, and his voice was like the sound of many waters. In his right hand he held seven stars, and from his mouth came a sharp, two-edged sword, and his face was like the sun shining with full force. (Revelation 1:12–16)

We finish these passages as we began them, with a symbolic vision of the Lord in glory—'one like a son of man' (as in Daniel 7:13–14, NIV). As Ezekiel fell on his face (1:28) and Isaiah cried 'Woe is me!' (6:5), so John admits, 'I fell at his feet as though dead' (Revelation 1:17). That is the only humanly possible response and, as we saw in a previous reading, in the presence of Almighty God, even the very heavens and the earth itself flee away.

'Seven' signifies completeness; white hair signifies the wisdom and authority that is the fruit of age; his eyes flash with what we would call the laser light of insight; the sword is double-edged, a lethal weapon. When we read that his face is 'like the sun shining with full force', we should think of the fiery heat of the noon sun in the southern Mediterranean or Turkey rather than the watery glow of a northern European summer.

Immediately afterwards, however, we have the profound

reassurance of the Holy One to the terrified mortal: 'Do not be afraid; I am the first and the last, and the living one. I was dead, and see, I am alive for ever and ever' (vv. 17–18). That is the paradox of our faith right there: the Lord of heaven, blazing in full splendour, still comes close to soothe our fears and touch us with his eternal love.

— Reflection and prayer —

*'Amen. Come, Lord Jesus!' (Revelation 22:20)*

# New Daylight

Sustaining your daily journey with the Bible

## Edited by Sally Welch

*New Daylight* is BRF's most popular series of Bible reaing notes. Each edition provides four months of daily Bible readings and comment, with a regular team of contributors drawn from a range of church backgrounds.

*New Daylight* covers a varied selection of Old and New Testament, biblical themes, characters and seasonal readings. Each day offers a short Bible passage (text included), thought-provoking comment and a prayer or point for reflection, and aims to give a fresh, devotional approach to Bible reading.

These notes are ideal for anybody wanting an accessible yet stimulating aid to spending time with God each day, deepening their faith and knowledge of scripture.

Available in print (both standard and Deluxe format), as an app for Android, iPhone an iPad, and as a daily email.

*Standard and Deluxe print editions are available from your local Christian bookshop. Alternatively, visit www.biblereadingnotes.org. uk/new-daylight for full details and sample readings.*

# Acts
## The People's Bible Commentary

### Loveday Alexander

Acts is the story of the birth of the church and the beginnings of its journey around the world. The author, Luke, traces this journey from an upstairs room in Jerusalem through the travels of a host of individual disciples across the Mediterranean world, spreading the gospel wherever they go. It is also the story of the journey of faith: one of Luke's favourite metaphors for discipleship is 'the Way'. As we read, we share the excitement of those first Christians in finding that God is 'out there', waiting to meet and surprise them in the world.

*ISBN 978 1 84101 216 2    £8.99*
*Available from your local Christian bookshop or direct from BRF: please visit www.brfonline.org.uk*

# Confidence in the Living God
## David and Goliath revisited

### Andrew Watson

Using the story of David and Goliath, Andrew Watson takes a narrative theology approach to show how the Lord can be our confidence, whatever the odds. He explores how God can develop a proper self-confidence within individuals and his church, revealing the gospel through transforming words and transformed lives.

He considers, too, how we can confidently tackle the challenges of day-to-day living, whether a difficult work situation or family relationship, or simply anxiety about the future. The book includes a study guide and is ideal as a whole church course on the subject of confidence.

*ISBN 978 0 85746 482 8     £7.99*
*Available from your local Christian bookshop or direct from BRF: please visit www.brfonline.org.uk*

# Deep Calls to Deep
## Spiritual formation in the hard places of life

### Tony Horsfall

The Psalms offer honest insights into the reality of life with God, reflecting every human emotion and situation. Through looking at some of the psalms written 'from the depths', we can understand more fully the way in which God is at work to shape our characters and form the life of Christ within us during difficult times.

This book offers reflections drawn from selected psalms to guide us as we begin to make sense of our own history with God, and also point us to how we can get to know God better here and now, preparing us for whatever may lie ahead.

*ISBN 978 1 84101 731 0      £7.99*
*Available from your local Christian bookshop or direct from BRF: please visit www.brfonline.org.uk*

# Believe in Miracles

## A spiritual journey of positive change

### Carmel Thomason

*Believe in Miracles* is a 40-day journey into a world of possibility. Focusing on small practical steps, you are invited to follow a series of short exercises that will help bring about lasting changes in your life, leading to a more prayerful, contented and connected state of being. By looking for the good and focusing on actions to take now, you will learn to view differently your daily circumstances, your relationship with God, and your relationships with others, bringing something of the ways of heaven to earth.

*ISBN 978 0 85746 420 0      £8.99*
*Available from your local Christian bookshop or direct from BRF: please visit www.brfonline.org.uk*

# Moments of Grace
## Reflections on meeting with God

### Joy MacCormick

From desolation to celebration, loneliness to love, *Moments of Grace* offers pithy, thought-provoking reflections on themes connecting God, faith and the journey of life. Questions for further pondering help the reader make links between head and heart, between what they believe, what they wrestle with believing and what they experience day by day.

Joy MacCormick has written this book to help people have a closer encounter with God in prayer, especially those who may struggle to find a place in conventional church worship.

*ISBN 978 0 85746 224 4     £6.99*
*Available from your local Christian bookshop or direct from BRF: please visit www.brfonline.org.uk*

# Encountering the Risen Christ

### From Easter to Pentecost:
### the message of the resurrection
### and how it can change us

## Mark Bradford

How can we encounter the risen Lord Jesus in a life-transforming way? How can we be equipped and strengthened to share the message of the resurrection with the world?

The post-resurrection encounters between Jesus and the disciples provide us with some of the most profound and personal moments to be found in scripture. The risen Christ comes to his disciples in all their brokenness—their sadness, fear, doubt, shattered dreams and failure—and calls them to a future filled with hope, confidence, confirmed faith, new beginnings and restored lives.

*Encountering the Risen Christ* reflects on the main characters in the post-resurrection accounts and shows how we too can encounter Jesus Christ in a life-transforming way.

*ISBN 978 0 85746 428 6     £7.99*
*Available from your local Christian bookshop or direct from BRF: please visit www.brfonline.org.uk*

# Postcards from Heaven

### Words and pictures
### to help you hear from God

## Ellie Hart

'My heart's desire is that this book could become a place where you can encounter our wonderful, beautiful, untameable, passionate, loving God and hear him speak directly to you, whatever your circumstances.'

Writer and artist Ellie Hart has created a series of 'postcards from heaven'— her own paintings linked to short, thought-provoking reflections, to help all who long to hear more clearly from God, especially when going through seasons of change and uncertainty.

*ISBN 978 0 85746 427 9     £7.99*

*Available from your local Christian bookshop or direct from BRF: please visit www.brfonline.org.uk*

# Journalling the Bible

## 40 writing exercises

### Corin Child

The spiritual discipline of journalling has become increasingly popular in recent years and this book shows how it can furitfully overlap with creative writing to provide an original way of engaging with the Bible.

'Bible study' is usually taken to mean 'reading and discussing', but writing offers a different way of interacting with the text, generating new insights and application even from the most familiar of passages. *Journalling the Bible* offers 40 writing/journalling exercises that have been tested in workshops around the country, providing an imaginative resource for individual and group work.

*ISBN 978 0 84101 736 5     £7.99*

*Available from your local Christian bookshop or direct from BRF: please visit www.brfonline.org.uk*

# Encircling the Christian Year

## Liturgies and reflections
## for the seasons of the Church

### Barbara Mosse

The seasons of the Church's year parallel those of the natural world, gifting us with opportunities for spiritual life and growth. The watchfulness of Advent with its symbolism of light and darkness gives way to the explosion of joy as we welcome the birth of Christ; the sombre season of Lent leads us through the despair of the cross to the wonder and joy of Easter. The weeks of 'Ordinary Time' encourage us to persist in our walk with Christ during those times when nothing much seems to be happening.

*Encircling the Christian Year* presents a series of short liturgies for each week of the Church calendar, including a Bible reading, reflection and prayers, suitable for both individual and small group use. The book invites us to deeper prayer, to grow in our relationship with the God who loves us and accompanies us through all the seasons of our lives.

*ISBN 978 0 85746 045 5     £9.99*

*Available from your local Christian bookshop or direct from BRF: please visit www.brfonline.org.uk*

# Enjoyed
## this book?

**Write a review**—we'd love to hear what you think.
Email: reviews@brf.org.uk

**Keep up to date**—receive details of our new books as they happen.
Sign up for email news and select your interest groups at:
www.brfonline.org.uk/findoutmore/

### Follow us on Twitter @brfonline

**By post**—to receive new title information by post (UK only), complete the form below and post to: BRF Mailing Lists, 15 The Chambers, Vineyard, Abingdon, Oxfordshire, OX14 3FE

| **Your Details** |
| --- |
| Name _____ |
| Address_____ |
| _____ |
| Town/City _____ Post Code _____ |
| Email _____ |

| **Your Interest Groups** (*Please tick as appropriate) |
| --- |

- ❏ Advent/Lent
- ❏ Bible Reading & Study
- ❏ Children's Books
- ❏ Discipleship
- ❏ Leadership
- ❏ Messy Church
- ❏ Pastoral
- ❏ Prayer & Spirituality
- ❏ Resources for Children's Church
- ❏ Resources for Schools

### Support your local bookshop
Ask about their new title information schemes.